LEAVING THE CONFEDERATE CLOSET

A Southern Lesbian's Journey

BONNIE R. STRICKLAND

More acclaim for Bonnie R. Strickland's

LEAVING THE CONFEDERATE CLOSET
A Southern Lesbian's Journey

What a joy to read this book ... I learned about growing up in the south; some will learn about growing up as a woman and a lesbian. Others will marvel at how early adversity can be overcome and end in personal success. But every reader will learn something.

Charles Silverstein, Ph.D
Committee on Ethical Practice, NYSPA LGBT Taskforce,
NYSPA Gold Medal for Achievement in Psychology,
APF Fellow, American Psychological Association
Author, *The Joy of Gay Sex*

Reading Leaving the Confederate Closet *is a rare pleasure of sitting with a distinguished elder in the field of LGBTQ+ psychology and listening to her life story ... She recounts significant friendships and lovers, pioneering steps in civil rights as well as lesbian and gay liberation, and a lifelong struggle with bi-polar depression.*

Douglas C. Kimmel, Ph.D
Professor Emeritus City College, CUNY; Co-founder SAGE: Advo-
cacy & Services for LGBT Elders; Founding Member and Historian,
American Psychological Association, Division 44: Society for the
Psychology of Sexual Orientation and Gender Diversity

At times funny, joyful, poignant, and optimistic, Leaving the Confederate Closet *is a must read. It is a highly compelling story of one of our powerful, beloved pioneers in psychology.*

Melba J. T. Vasquez, Ph.D, ABPP
Former president, American Psychological Association

This book is the story of a lesbian psychologist's journey of strength and resilience in the move toward personal liberation.

Arlene Noriega, Ph.D
Past president, American Psychological Association (APA),
Division 44: Society for the Psychology of Sexual Orientation and
Gender Diversity; Representative to the Council of the APA,
Division 44: Society for the Psychology of Sexual Orientation and
Gender Diversity; Council Leadership Team Member-At-Large

Leaving the Confederate Closet *is the remarkable life story of a humble, brilliant, accomplished woman ... I am telling my friends and colleagues all – You will love this book from start to finish.*

Ellen Cole, Ph.D
Professor of Psychology at Russell Sage College
Author, *Older Women Who Work*

Full reviews begin on page 237

Cover photo by Marjorie Nott
Author photo by Douglas Kimmel

Cover and book design by Cindy Casey

Published by
CCE PUBLISHING
Edgewater, Florida
CindyCaseyEditing.com

Printed in the United States of America

ISBN 978-0-578-99899-2

LEAVING THE CONFEDERATE CLOSET

A Southern Lesbian's Journey

BONNIE R. STRICKLAND

CCE PUBLISHING

Dedication

To family and friends, especially Marjorie.

Contents

CONTENTS continued ...

Contents ... *continued*

Prologue

A small, tattered Confederate flag sits on my desk where I see it every day. I have had it since my high school days but I am not sure why I keep it. Perhaps it simply reminds me of where I came from and the long journey to where I am now. However, I suspect the reasons are not that simple and are as complex as the southern culture that spawned me. I grew up in the South torn across boundaries of Black and white, male and female, pride and shame, hospitality and hate.

Raised in a southern city distinguished by the vehemence of its violence and the "Redneck Riviera" of the panhandle of northwest Florida, how did I find my way to the urbane, sophisticated, gentle Pioneer Valley of Western Massachusetts? The first of my family to go to college, how could I become a professor in a major university? Reared in racism and steeped in religion, how was I able to join a scholarly world dedicated to humane values and the freedom of ideas? Immersed in an extended family of more cousins than I could count, none of whom went to college, what prepared me to read and write and study alone among the Yankees of whom I had always been suspicious? Most of all how did the dark secret of being different, of crossing sexualities and sin and salvation shape my life?

Sitting at my desk on a wintery morning in New England at eighty-five years old, I marvel at how I came to be half a century, two thousand miles and thirty degrees from home.

Chapter 1
Perhaps it Begins with Family

Ask a Southerner what time it is and he or she will tell you how to build a clock. We are storytellers, reaching perhaps too far in the past to inform the present. We grow up with a powerful sense of place and fierce loyalties to family. This is my story, telling it as best I can.

I don't think in her heart of hearts that she really meant to kill me. But then my pretty, vivacious mother (I always called her Mama) wasn't very good at following through on her intentions, whatever they may have been. When things didn't go her way, she would simply blame others. As a toddler, I pulled the trigger of a loaded shotgun I found in my maternal grandparents' living room and tore a hole in the ceiling. Mama blamed Uncle Jennings for leaving the gun there. She would have said it was not her fault that the bull got loose from a fenced pasture and tried to gore me. Still a toddler, a yard baby now, no longer a lap baby, I was alone outside in the backyard of my grandparents' farm. Hearing the noise when the bull hit the back wall with his horns, with me between them, my grandmother raced from the kitchen waving her apron at the bull as he was backing up for another shot at me. Mama was behind her crying.

I do not know who Mama could have blamed when she took me in the deep end of a swimming pool when neither of us could swim. We both went under and had to be rescued. Maybe she had her eye on the handsome lifeguard who jumped in to save us. She was always attracted to good-looking men. It seems that from an early age, I knew I could not trust Mama to keep me safe. In fact, I would have to protect her and eventually thought that of all the women I would love. I knew even then that I never wanted to be weak like her.

Goodness knows Mama should have been strong. She came from a long line of independent forebears who settled the river swamps in the panhandle of northwest Florida. Her maternal grandfather was Benjamin Thomas Lanier. While the name is French, the Lanier ancestors lived in England and some were musicians in the English court. The Lanier family boasted a number of famous folks, including Confederate heroes who fought in the Civil War or the War of Northern Aggression, as we preferred to call it.

I was to hear of their valor, and that of my paternal great-grandfather, through most of my growing up days. On long, hot summer evenings, we kids would sit on a porch and listen to a great aunt or uncle tell stories. Conveniently ignoring the fact that I was female, I decided I wanted to be a soldier and fight for the Confederacy if it were to rise again.

The stories I remember the best were the exploits of my great-great uncle, Charles Malcolm Lanier. He was a skilled horseman and is said to have trained Robert E. Lee's horse, Traveler. Once when captured by the Yankees, he waged a bet with them that he could ride at full speed and pick up a handkerchief from the ground. When asked to demonstrate, he took off on a gallop, raced right by the handkerchief, and escaped.

My paternal great grandfather, John Strickland, fought in five campaigns for the Confederacy. He was mustered out when wounded by a musket ball as he was drinking from a creek at Chickamauga. His family could be traced to five Strickland brothers who settled in the southeastern United States after they were released from prison in England with the promise that they would never return.

Back to my mother's side. A family secret is that Benjamin Lanier, her grandfather, left his pregnant wife and ran off with her sister. They traveled from Tupelo, Mississippi to Eufaula, Alabama where my great grandfather worked on riverboats as an alleged "doctor." My grandmother, Rosalee Estella (Essie) was the first child of this union followed by several more siblings. Eufaula was a bustling city of merchants and planters perched on the Apalachicola River, the boundary between Alabama and Georgia that separated the more civilized Southeast and the wilderness of the West. It was established on Indian land and certain treaties were written. Eufaula grew so quickly, however, that the town soon expanded beyond its borders; the treaties were broken. The indigenous people, predominantly Cherokee and Muscogee, were resettled in Oklahoma via way of the "Trail of Tears."

After a few years, my maternal great grandfather and great grandmother moved down the river to Apalachicola, Florida, where the river flows into the Gulf. Apalach, as it is known, was then the third busiest cotton port in the country. My great grandparents ran a hotel, frequented primarily by folks from the riverboats, especially the gamblers. When she was fifteen, their daughter, my grandmother, Essie, eloped over the balcony of the hotel and ran off with Albert Gregory. This was a short-term union. At 18, she married a farmer, Felix Brown, and had several children with him. After Mr. Brown died, my grandmother then married my grandfather, Joseph Weldon Whitfield, a widower with several children. He died when I was two and I know less about him. I was told that he lost both of his parents in a carriage accident and was raised by neighbors.

My mother, Willie Perdita Whitfield, was the twelfth of thirteen living children of this blended family who had settled into a small community called Dalkeith. Born in 1916, she was raised in the river swamps of the panhandle of Florida.

Her father, my grandfather, worked on the river cutting cypress logs and tending apiaries. With an abundance of tupelo trees, he and my great uncles established the tupelo honey business – a honey that does not granulate and is still very popular in health food stores. My grandfather's main source of income, however, was making bootleg whiskey – moonshine - from stills hidden on the river. So protective was he of the business that, with my Uncle Cliff, he shot and killed a man who was "messing around" with one of the stills. I was told that Uncle Cliff actually pulled the trigger but my grandfather took the blame for the killing. This led to their convictions and jail, my grandfather for thirteen years and Uncle Cliff for three.

During World War II, Uncle Cliff engaged in all sorts of illegal activities, such as importing untaxed whiskey from Cuba. He was able to secure things, such as nylon and rubber tires, that for everyone else were rationed by the war effort and unavailable. He continued to traffic in illegal whiskey, and occasionally, I would accompany him on his deliveries to the piney woods. He would locate his payment, usually in the crotch of a branch in an agreed upon tree, and exchange it for a jar of moonshine.

In the late 1940s, when he was 39, he confronted a man with whom he had some sort of disagreement. Uncle Cliff pulled out a gun but the man responded quickly, shot and killed him. Several others of my aunts and uncles and cousins also died unexpectedly usually by drowning on the river or by gunshot wounds. At one time, I counted fifteen of my extended family to die violently.

One such drowning was my Aunt May, the first child of my maternal grandmother. Aunt May fell in love with my Uncle Joe, the first son from my grandfather's previous first marriage. Although they were not related by blood, their parents were opposed to their romance. I am told that one of my uncles brought home a baby that had been given to him by someone on a riverboat. This was not that unusual during those days. Children lost parents to early deaths and were sometimes raised by strangers. However, my grandmother found my Aunt May nursing the baby and determined that it belonged to her and my Uncle Joe. They eventually married and had four children.

Uncle Joe kept bees on the river. One winter night he was returning from the apiary with his family when the boat hit a submerged log. All were tossed into the water. Aunt May handed up each child to Uncle Joe who had found land. As she delivered the last child, she sank under the water and drowned. Her body was recovered down river thirty-two days later. Mama said she still remembers the heavy wool sweater that May was wearing that likely pulled her under. Their youngest son, who was rescued that night, was to face yet another tragedy as an adult. He was cleaning his shotgun when his wife came into the room. The gun went off accidentally and she was killed.

Another instance occurred when my second cousin, Dwayne, then about thirteen, was returning on the river from a day of squirrel hunting with a friend. The river was high and he saw a dog stranded on an island. He rescued the dog and put it in the boat. When Dwayne started the motor, the scared dog jumped around and hit the shotgun, which was lying in the bottom. The safety was not on; the gun went off and killed Dwayne instantly.

My cousin, Billy, loved the river and lived close to it all his life. He built a small houseboat and anchored it to a bank so he could retreat into the deep river swamps to fish and to hunt. One winter night after he had arrived at the houseboat, one of his boats became loose and began floating away. Billy jumped into the water to retrieve it. He caught up with it but could not hold on. He sank beneath the water and drowned.

In the midst of this rough and rowdy family, Mama grew up, attractive, sparkling, sociable and likely spoiled. Instead of Willie, she opted to be called Billie, a name that stayed with her throughout her life. She had dark brown hair, deep brown eyes and was very pretty both as a child and as an adult. She learned to slop hogs and milk cows but was much more inclined to parties and sneaking off to date at an early age.

She was very popular. One of my uncles remarked, "She lit up a room when she entered."

School was not her strength and she dropped out in the tenth grade. I am told that she was expelled in the fourth grade when she tried to set the school on fire. As was the case back then, few of her brothers and sisters finished high school.

Of my fifty-some cousins, only my brother, Roy, always known as Bud, and I went to college. We both had a professional or doctoral degree by age twenty-five, him a dentist and me a psychologist.

It is hard to know what differentiated the two of us from the numerous cousins. I do know Mama was always pushing Bud and me to be successful, whether at school or in sports. She even had me take piano lessons, an unlikely undertaking for a tomboy from a poor family. I suspect, however, that our differences emerged primarily in that Bud and I attended public schools in Birmingham, which were quite good. Cousins had only the rather impoverished schools of a rural community.

Bud and I were exposed early to subjects such as music, art and drama. We also had easy access to a public library that was quite extensive in its holdings. Cousins were in very small classes without opportunities for extended offerings. In the Birmingham schools, my brother and I learned about the possibility of college, whereas the cousins were not expected to be college bound.

The few ways for poor children to escape the poverty of the South were through education, athletics or the military. The rural schools of northwest Florida could not provide adequate education or emphasize educational opportunities; they were too small to field athletic teams. Almost all of my male cousins joined the military and my female cousins married military men. Interestingly, the five cousins closest to my age, who I played with growing up, have returned to live close to the old home place. Two are deceased but each of the others is still married to his or her first spouse now going on some sixty years.

After he was released from jail, my maternal grandfather, Weldon Whitfield, ran the post office and a small general store in Dalkeith. He bought merchandise and supplies from manufacturers in the North. Mama would often travel, usually with brothers and sisters, to secure shoes and apparel for the store.

On one of her trips to Birmingham, she went to a party hosted by her next oldest sister, Aunt Verna, who was dating Roy Strickland, a handsome young man from Birmingham. Mama took one look at him, as he did her, and it was love at first sight. They married three weeks later. Some time passed and they took a second look realizing that the relationship was in trouble.

Their early days of marriage could not have been easy. Mama was sixteen and Daddy six years older. It was 1934, the depths of the Great Depression. Daddy was jobless and at first, they lived with his family in Birmingham. This was indeed difficult in that his mother, my grandmother, never fully accepted Mama. In fact, at one point, Mama awoke to find my grandmother leaning over the bed with a knife threatening to kill her. Daddy intervened.

My grandmother, Ida Ruth Lee, from whom I received my middle name, suffered from what was then called "nervous breakdowns." She would tear off her clothes and go running through the neighborhood until apprehended and taken to an asylum. She would then recover and return home. Now we would diagnose her illness as bi-polar or schizoaffective disorder, a condition that we were to learn would pass down through generations. She died two months before I was born, but I was welcomed with great joy by the men in the family.

When I was an infant, Mama and Daddy lived in my paternal grandfather's home. Then Daddy found a job in Louisville where we lived until moving back to Birmingham when I was four. At first, we lived my grandfather Strickland. Then, as had been the case in Louisville, we lived in rented apartments with small rooms and cast off furniture. When I was an infant, my bed was a dresser drawer as was Bud's later on. Daddy was always promising Mama that they would eventually have their own home, but that was not to be.

Daddy was the second of three sons. His father, John Griffin Strickland, had a job on the railroad, an occupation that Daddy was to take up when he finally found work during World War II. Because transportation was essential for the war effort, Daddy was able to escape the draft. His older brother, John, also worked on the railroad before he was drafted into the Army. Daddy's younger brother, Charles, eventually took a job in a steel factory. They all finished high school. My paternal grandmother was a Lee and made certain the initials R. E. were passed on to my father, Roy Elkins, and eventually my brother.

FAMILY

Clockwise from top: Daddy records information in a log book for his railroad job; Bonnie with Mama and Bud; Bonnie holding Bud; and Bonnie as a toddler.

Above: Mama, Bud and Bonnie.
Below: Bonnie's maternal grandmother, Essie Lanier Whitfield.
Right: Aunt Edna cooking on the
river bank.

Chapter 2
Early Days

Mama and Daddy fell easily into a stereotypical marriage. He was to be the breadwinner and she was the dutiful homemaker. They were eager to have children, especially a boy. Two years after they married, I came along. Evidently, Mama had a long and difficult labor – the length of which became longer each time she told the story of my birth. I am sure we could be famous in some medical archives. The doctor finally said that he could not save us both. I was delivered with forceps and pulled without breathing into the world. A nurse dipped me in cold and then in hot water, the highest technology of 1936. I eventually took my first breath.

Mama said that when she awoke, Daddy was at the end of her bed cradling me in his arms. My face was red and swollen from the forceps. Mama recalls that she asked, "What is it?" and Daddy responded, "It's a little girl." My disappointed Mama reminded him that he had wanted a boy. He remarked that he didn't know I was going to be so pretty. Pretty I was not, but my delusional Daddy treated me as if I were his only child. He was not even present when Bud was born some four years later.

In those early years, I know there were times that Mama loved and comforted me. I am sure I was desperate for her affection, looking for it at every turn. However, what I recall most is confusion. Although she could be warm and affectionate, I never knew quite what was going to happen. Once when I was a toddler, I walked across the room and bit her as far up as I could reach on her thigh. She quickly took her hand and slammed me across the room – my first lesson in learning that an aggressive act on my part would be met with a fierce explosion of retaliation from her.

Some of the time, however, was filled with closeness. Mama

dressed me in frilly clothes and provided me with toys, especially dolls. I recall holding her hand and walking with her to the alleged toy hospital to repair one of my favorite dolls. In some ways, I think I was like a doll to her.

I suspect she delighted in attending to me, curling my hair, and presenting me to the world as her adored child. When she would take a nap in the afternoons, I would lie beside her and run my fingers through her hair. I imagine at that time that Mama turned to me for affection and intimacy as Daddy was increasingly absent. However, Mama's attention to me waned abruptly with the birth of my brother. Sensing this, perhaps my first act of rebellion was sucking my thumb, an activity Mama abhorred and discouraged at every turn. She was continually scolding me but I was relentless in my defiance. I sucked my thumb until I was seven or eight years old.

One day everything changed for me. Mama placed a dark haired infant in the middle of the bed and announced that he was home to stay and he was to have my bottle. She maintained that there was only one bottle and now it was his.

Although she had little to leave me when she died, I did find instructions about my initial feeding that she had kept for all of her life. These came from the public health nurse who visited and likely welcomed by Mama who needed all the help she could get as a new mother. The listing recommended feedings six times daily, included the formula (evaporated milk, detra maltose #1 and boiled water) and how to care for the bottles and nipples. I continued to drink from a bottle until I was four and my brother arrived.

When my brother came home, Mama told me that he was to have the bottle and it was no longer available to me. Enraged by its loss, I would sneak around and try to take the bottle from him, putting my hand over his mouth to hush his crying. One day, the visiting health nurse, who recognized the situation, told Mama to give me back a bottle. She retrieved one from the top of a cabinet. I realized that there had always been more than one bottle. I knew then that Mama had not been truthful with me. Likely, this was the beginning of my mistrust of her. The reclaimed bottle, however, was not nearly as satisfying as I remembered - the taste of milk mingled with her deception.

At last, Mama and Daddy had the beloved boy. At that time of his birth, I felt confused and abandoned. What had I done to elicit this exile? Now I was in an unfamiliar and uncaring world. Later, I would envy his place in the family as I felt increasingly ostracized. Mama, thrilled with this boy child, especially seemed to favor him; I was more of an afterthought. Daddy seemed more even in his acceptance of us both but I always felt that he was more comfortable with me.

My memory of Daddy is less intense than that of Mama. He worked on the railroad and was not home as often as she was. I remember that one time Mama took me to the railroad station to see him. He lifted me up into the cab of the train and let me blow the whistle. It was exhilarating. I also remember a special time when we were living in Louisville where he was working on the Louisville and Nashville railroad. He and I walked over to nearby Churchill Downs and sat quietly together in the empty stands. It is the only time that I can remember when it was just the two of us. I also recall that once when my Mama and Daddy were drinking their breakfast coffee, I asked if I could have some. Mama immediately said no but Daddy, letting me be more adventurous, gave me some of his. The coffee was hot and bitter; I have never liked coffee since.

My main recollection of that early time was mostly of the continued traveling between Birmingham and Dalkeith. Mama was forever leaving Daddy to go to Florida to be with her mother and siblings and then returning. There were many bus trips and another incident occurred which led me to once again question whether Mama could keep me safe.

On one trip, likely exhausted from holding a bouncing baby girl on her lap, she handed me over to a stranger, a soldier, across the aisle. At first, I was warm in his arms but then he began to fondle me. All of my feelings of comfort evaporated. Mama also blamed me for one of her miscarriages that occurred on a bus trip. She told me it happened because I kept jumping up and down in her lap.

Early on, I was learning that hers was not always the supportive, encouraging behavior that I so desperately craved. Once, when I was quite small, Daddy's older brother, my Uncle John, and I were acting out a play. We had socks on our hands and were pretending they were people. Mama came by and asked what we were doing. I explained, but she rather severely responded that indeed these were only socks.

I know now how lucky I was to have my Uncle John at least for a while. A single, sensitive man, he would read to me and take me to ball games where his younger brother, my uncle, was playing. I lost him early, however, when he was drafted into World War II. After five months of basic training, he was instructed to take his rifle apart and then reassemble it. He refused to do so. He also refused to speak to anyone. He was discharged and returned to a psychiatric ward at the Veterans Administration Hospital in Alabama. Although occasionally he would leave the hospital, and at one point lived with us, he never really recovered from his paranoid schizophrenia.

In addition to Uncle John, I also was lucky to have my Mama's extended family. When we would return to Dalkeith, my grandmother, aunts and uncles would treat me as if I were theirs. I became just another one of the many children.

Chapter 3
Florida Life

In Dalkeith, my maternal grandparents owned considerable acreage on the Lockee Lakes, which were sloughs off the Apalachicola and Chipola rivers. They lived in what was a typical Florida cracker house, with a general store and post office in front of it. After my grandparents died, my Mama's youngest sister, Aunt Edna, and her husband, Uncle Jennings, lived in the house along with their five children.

Early on, the house was in pretty good shape. Through the years, however, it began to fall into disarray and the store and post office were demolished. Occasionally, Uncle Jennings and his son, Charles, would take off into the piney woods to find a site for another house. They would even set the four corners of the foundation. Then something like hunting season would interrupt and they would leave the concrete blocks behind.

I loved being in Florida, in the northwest panhandle. As Mama was always returning to Dalkeith, my brother, Bud, and I spent considerable time there especially before we began school in Birmingham. In the summer, the heat was oppressive, but we were used to it.

Indoor plumbing, electricity and air conditioning were a long time away. The house had a wide hall – a dogtrot – from front to back with two rooms on each side. As you entered on the left, there was a living room with a large fireplace that heated the house. The other three rooms were bedrooms with a small extension of a dining room off the back.

The kitchen was detached from the house and connected via a plank to the small dining area. It had a large cook stove that burned wood and heated water for outdoor baths each week in a number 2 wash tub. The pump for water, which often had to be primed, was outside. Drinking water was brought into the kitchen in a pan with a metal dipper. A smoke house to cure meat was in the back yard and an outhouse was off to the side. Even though there were slop jars in the bedrooms, it was expected that one would go to the outhouse if possible, even on cold winter nights.

Light was provided from kerosene lamps, but we usually went to bed early, sleeping on dusty, thin cotton mattresses. There were no screens on the windows but they did have wooden shutters. On hot summer evenings, the windows would be shut and bug spray pumped throughout the house to kill the mosquitoes. It's a wonder we were not killed as well, asphyxiated in our beds.

The dirt front yard was always swept clean in front of a porch that also had a small room on it. This room contained an old upright piano that eventually fell through the floor. No one did anything about it. We kids could no longer reach the keyboard but we could reach down and strum the strings attached to the keys. The back wall of one of the bedrooms collapsed and was never repaired. Chickens and other critters wandered through the dogtrot that was open at both ends. Sometimes the chickens would lay eggs in the house making it convenient to gather them. Their poop was not so easy to clean up.

My cousins and I were early engaged in the household chores. My favorite was grubbing worms. Uncle Jennings would wake us before dawn. We would pile into the back of his pickup truck and go out to the palmetto fields. Uncle Jennings would drive a two by four into the ground and rub over it with another piece of wood. The ground would vibrate and earthworms would climb to the surface. We kids would run around, pick them up, and place them in tin cans that Uncle Jennings would then deliver to various bait stores. We always had a great time. We were outside; we were together. Although unexpressed, we were pleased to be of help and knew we were contributing to the family. Everyone had responsibilities and this was one of the fun ones.

Other chores included slopping the hogs and feeding the chickens. My grandmother taught me how to wring a chicken's neck, a skill for which I have little use these days. Early on, I learned to scale fish. I swept the dirt front yard and sometimes emptied the slop jars.

I loved being outside and would eagerly run to meet Uncle Jennings when he would return from the river usually with fish or small game from hunting. Occasionally, he came home with a deer he had slaughtered. Once he delivered a turtle so large it almost covered the back of his pickup truck. It supposedly had the taste of seven different kinds of meat or fowl. I don't remember what they all were. Aunt Edna would cook pieces of the turtle and serve it to us as part of a meal. Mama did not like it but the rest of us found it yummy.

Another exotic species that Uncle Jennings hunted was alligators. He would poach gators in the swamp, bring them home, salt their skins in the smokehouse, and then sell the skins. I vividly recall one time when he brought home a slew of baby gators in a washtub. They were hissing and biting with already sharp teeth. When Uncle Jennings was not looking, my cousins and I would poke sticks at the baby gators to see them snap at them.

Uncle Jennings also collected poisonous snakes to sell to various laboratories where the venom could be extracted. We kids were always curious about what Uncle Jennings might bring home; we would gather around to see his latest treasure. He was always careful to keep us safe. He was particularly concerned about the snakes that he kept in sturdy wire cages. We could see them but were not to get close.

Most of all, I loved going into the swamps and onto the river. I learned to fish and could have been involved in hunting, but I did not like the idea of killing wild creatures.

At night, my cousins and I would sometimes go frog gigging – that is we would find frogs and spear them. We would float in a boat close to the shore and beam a light across the bank. At times, the light would be reflected in large eyes and we knew that was a gator. At other times, the eyes were small and we knew that was frog. We would approach and gig the frog with a three-pronged spear and put it in a burlap bag. Aunt Edna would then cook up the frog legs the next day.

At times, we would have cookouts of fish and hush puppies on the river landing. At one of these, my cousin Billy who was about six or seven, yelled to his father, my Uncle Jennings, that he had stepped on a snake. I assumed that Uncle Jennings would want Billy to escape, but instead he yelled for Billy to keep standing on it so he could catch it and add it to his collection.

Our lives revolved around water. Dalkeith was only twenty miles from the Gulf of Mexico and occasionally some of the grown-ups would drive as many cousins as were around to the beach. The sand there is like sugar, fine and white. There were few homes or buildings on the beach. We usually had it to ourselves. We would paddle around in the surf and scamper through the bays feeling for oysters with our bare feet. We would float face down looking for scallops. Finally, exhausted, we would head back home.

The times I remember best were middle childhood when I spent long lazy days alone in the river swamps. I would walk barefoot on the hot sand down a sandy path to the water, slapping at the ever present mosquitoes. I would pick blackberries, warm from the sun, and eat them along the way. There was always an extra boat, a flat-bottomed bateaux, at the landing. I would carefully settle a 22 rifle in the bottom of the boat, along with a cane pole and some worms. Maybe I would fish a little but mostly I would float with my fantasies. I would watch the sun slant through the Spanish moss into the murky water, lighting the dust motes so they danced like golden flakes. Jesus bugs walked on the water. Bees swarmed around bright blossoms. Long legged cranes and herons scattered through the palmettos dipping their beaks for fish. Lazy turtles sunned themselves on fallen logs. I knew every slough and waterway.

I day dreamed that the cypress knees and tupelo trees were ornamental hedges on the liquid lawn of the house that I would eventually build. All of my uncles built their homes near the river. I assumed I would do the same. Like them, I would live off the land – well, at least the water.

Life was simple and I was involved in every aspect of the ordinary. I remember steering Uncle Jennings' pickup truck on the dirt road in front of the house, the metallic taste of water from the dipper in the kitchen, the briny smell of the smokehouse, the oily scent of the kerosene lamps, the almost overpowering bug spray and the faint stench of the hog pen from across the yard. I recall turning over in bed to face the feet of a cousin since we slept head to toe. I remember the hot sand of the front yard under my bare feet and the women folks sitting on the porch shelling beans, getting ready for supper. I was at home in the peace of being securely in a place where I belonged.

Chapter 4
School Days

I started the first grade well ahead of my peers. Mama and Uncle John had taught me letters and numbers and I was already reading. I fell in love with my first grade teacher and determined right then that I would be a teacher when I grew up. I skipped the second grade but in every grade that I advanced, I reaffirmed that I would like to teach that age.

My obsession with school likely occurred because, along with the library, it became my home. The teachers were the parental figures I never had emotionally. I loved school, did well, and the teachers recognized my efforts. I was entered in several contests. I won prizes for spelling and for reciting poetry. In many ways, the public schools of Alabama were ahead of their time. In the fourth grade, we began to leave homeroom and attend classes in subjects other than reading, writing, and arithmetic. We took art, drama, music and gym. We were given our own instrument to play in music class. Along with home economics, I was allowed to take shop with the boys. The gym teacher was especially accommodating to me, even allowing me to put on boxing gloves and spar with another girl.

When I was in the fourth or fifth grade, an incident occurred that I have always remembered. I was in art class busily drawing a picture of a house. I was working hard to keep the lines straight and produce a perfect picture. The teacher came by and bent over the desk to see what I was drawing. She then took the crayon from my hand and scratched it over my straight lines. She said, "Draw beyond the lines." I was confused and thought I had done something wrong. It would be years before I took the matter to heart and realized what she was trying to tell me to expand, to be creative. Unfortunately, I continue to be too rule-bound and have trouble going beyond boundaries.

Life at school was steady and wonderful for me. Life at home was both chaotic and boring. I never knew what new scheme Mama had for me but in her absence at work, I was truly on my own. I escaped into school and books. However, my moods were generally dysphoric. I recall walking home from school one day and thinking that kids were supposed to be happy. I thought to myself that I would always remember feeling sad as a child. Perhaps this was the beginning of the bouts of depression that I experienced throughout my life. I also acquired some obsessive traits such as counting from the last car that passed when I wanted to cross the street.

In the fourth grade, the school provided me with a viola, which I was learning to play. Unfortunately, for my budding music career, that fall Mama took Bud and me to Chicago to live close to my Aunt Verna, Mama's next oldest sister, and her husband. Mama was always close to Aunt Verna and stayed closely connected to her. I think Mama moved us to Chicago to start some sort of new life near her sister.

During the War, Aunt Verna had joined the Women's Army Corp and met her husband, Bill, who was also in the service. Being in the military, they moved around a lot, but Mama always maintained close ties with them. They were warm and attentive to Bud and me and we would often spend vacations with them.

In Chicago, we moved into an apartment and to my delight, there was a library next door. I immediately got a library card and once again retreated to books. My school days in Chicago were relatively unpleasant. There were no music lessons or extracurricular activities. I made no friends. I had trouble understanding folks with their northern dialect. Aside from feeling like an outsider living among the Yankees, I also recall how windy and cold it was.

I do remember one bright spot. Mama took Bud and me to the Science and Technology museum. Along with the other exhibits, we supposedly descended through levels to a simulated coal mine. I was entranced.

Since we lived in the city in a very noisy neighborhood, there was little outdoor play. However, our second floor apartment was directly across the street from a movie theater. Saturday afternoons Bud and I would each spend a dime to go to the movies. Usually, there was a Western as well as cartoons and newsreels about the War.

Whatever Mama's dreams were about living in the North, maybe to start a new life, did not work out. We lasted no more than three or four months, returning to Birmingham before Christmas.

However, all of my stereotypes about Yankees had been reinforced. Folks were not friendly; they talked too fast and with an accent. I hated the noise, the cold, and the wind. I was thrilled to return to my elementary school and my friends. I happily reentered my classes although the viola was no longer available.

Looking back, I think I was raised by institutions, namely school, church, the library and the public parks. Aside from school, my other love was the public library across the street from our house. I had received my first library card when I was seven and began to read everything I could. I particularly enjoyed the summer programs when we were urged to read large numbers of books. Being my competitive self, I read everything in sight and won contests for having read the most books in the shortest amount of time.

Another institution that shaped my early being was the Southern Baptist Church. An added bonus was that we received credit on our school report card for attending church as did my Jewish friends who went to their services. No separation of church and state for us.

I was present every time the church opened its doors, including the regular Sunday morning, evening services, and Wednesday night prayer meetings. I attended the Baptist Training Union meetings and was a member of the Girls' Auxiliary, although I would have much preferred the boys' counterpart, namely the Royal Ambassadors.

The church also gave me a chance during the summers to attend Vacation Bible School. Here again, I was in my element and so competitive that I cheated on Bible drills. The church also sponsored summer trips to the mountains of North Carolina to attend religious retreats. I did not care so much for being indoors for the meetings, but I loved being outside.

While I could not become a preacher (they were all men), I was quite taken with the notion of becoming a missionary and traveling around the world to save the heathen. I had no idea why the heathen would want to become Southern Baptists, but I liked the idea of traveling.

The Southern Baptist Church was particularly strict on sin. This included dancing, drinking, smoking, swearing and any thoughts about sex. I learned that every kind of sexuality was sinful, whether of the spirit or flesh, except the missionary position in marriage.

Knowing that thoughts were not exempt and believing everything the preacher said, especially that sinning would relegate one to burning in everlasting hell, I fantasized a creature named Murdoch that lived within my head. He had a large, strong, metal cabinet with lots of drawers. Every time I had an impure thought, he would quickly put it in one of the drawers and lock it away.

Unfortunately, Murdoch was not quite quick enough for my stream of thoughts. I resigned myself to everlasting hell, this in spite of the fact that the whole of my rather limited sexual activities consisted of having been fondled by a soldier, a church deacon and the man who ran our neighborhood dry cleaner.

Virginity until marriage was expected; I determined to keep myself pure. Nothing was said about homosexuality, about which I knew little, but since it involved sexuality, I suspected it was also sinful.

Hell was literal with constant warnings that we would burn there if we were not proper Baptists. To escape this, I decided to join the church and accepted the call to Christ one Sunday morning. Later that day, I told Mama about my decision. She chided me for not letting her know in advance so that she could attend. It had simply not occurred to me that she would be interested.

Like other Baptist converts, I was dipped in the baptismal pool emerging to my newly acclaimed status as a church member. I would stay in my neighborhood church until I went off to college. There, I gave up all interest in the Baptist church and began to attend Unitarian meetings. This lasted through my college days.

I never did share things with Mama, or anyone else for that matter, like the confusion I felt when molested. In regard to the dry cleaning man, I had simply accepted that I was to take the dirty clothes to the cleaners not too far from our house. Even after he touched me, I assumed my responsibilities and continued to take the clothes in. His behavior was almost routine. I had no framework in which to understand it. Looking back now, I am surprised at my nonchalance. However, that was a time before one talked openly about sexual abuse. I had been raised to be a good child and respect my elders.

There was one time when I was about eleven or twelve that I may have been in real danger. I was returning home in the alley from some errand or other. A scruffy looking man began to follow me. Having been taught to be respectful to my elders, I worried that he would be offended if I ran from him. Still, I decided to run and looking back saw that he was running after me. Luckily, I had a head start and escaped into my house. Looking out the window, I saw that he had given up the chase and was leaving.

During these encounters, I was scared but my silent self never told anyone. I believed that I would have to be strong and keep everything inside. I felt like I could not depend on others to protect me but would have to fend for myself.

SCHOOL DAYS

School Days
1944 - 45

School Days
1947 - 1948

School Days
1951 - 1952

Above: Bonnie at age 4 or 5. Top: Bonnie's school portraits. Right: Bonnie says she's "in drag for some best-forgotten piano recital."

Chapter 5
Family Life

My parents' relationship had always been stormy. I remember when I was about six, Mama found Daddy with a woman in their bedroom. She tossed the woman's clothes out the window and chased her from the house. Mama was also enormously embarrassed when she contracted a sexually transmitted disease from my Dad. Many years later, when domestic abuse was talked about, I asked her if Daddy had ever hit her. She said no and remarked that if there had been one to perpetrate violence, it would have been her.

When I was seven, my parents divorced and Mama had to go to work. She was a single Mom before there was such a term. At first, my maternal grandmother took care of Bud and me. I don't remember much about her except that she seemed a formidable woman and a tough taskmaster. She was of small frame and looked like the quintessential grandmother with permed silver hair and flashing blue eyes. She was not affectionate, but rather stern and goal oriented, determined only to look after us and take care of the house. I do recall once, however, when she was bathing me, I said something about Mama. To my great surprise, my grandmother replied that my mother was a "piss ant." This was the first time I ever realized that Mama could have any flaws. I marveled at how my grandmother could be so swift and sure in her judgment.

I suspect my grandmother really ruled the house since Mama was working and away so much. I was scared of her and quick to obey her bidding, but she still whipped my brother and me for our various misbehaviors. These were usually small offenses like coming in late from playing or saying a cuss word. We would have to go and pick a switch from a bush outside and bring it to her. I always wondered what would hurt least -- to have the leaves remain on the switch or to strip it clean. I tried them both ways and both ways hurt.

Grandmother died in 1945 when I was nine. At her funeral, I saw Daddy tear up. It is the only time I ever saw him come close to crying or expressing any emotion. His strong silence had become a model of strength for me. I puzzled whether or not he could actually express any feelings. I did, however, further consider and reaffirm that his usual stoicism was the best approach to take in terms of dealing with my often-hysterical mother.

Mama had always been extremely close to her mother. Shortly after my grandmother's funeral, Mama told me that she had been speaking to her in the night. Mama cried. In one of those rare moments when she attempted to connect with me, she said she hoped that I would never have to know what it was like to be alone. I realized that even though my mother had family around and Bud and I were with her, we were not enough. She had been overly attached to her mother and did not find comfort in others. No wonder she felt helpless and alone. Less than thirty years old, she had two small children and was responsible for making a living for all of us without the support of her most dependable parent.

As I have mentioned, my impatient, easily distracted Mama was never very good at independent action. She was always dependent on the advice of others although she would not usually follow it. I began to realize this when I was about six. We were in one of the rented apartments in Birmingham and she showed me a tear stained letter from my Dad. After one of her escapes away, he had written begging her to come back to him. She asked me what she should do. Although I wanted to reply and to comfort her, I felt altogether helpless. First, I did not have the answer and secondly she was not likely to follow any advice I might give her.

Since Daddy was working on the railroad, he was not home a lot. When he was there he and Mama would fight. He would leave the house as often as he could. He would put fifty cents on top of the refrigerator to buy food although it was never enough. One evening I recall, after one of their fights, he took me into the one bedroom and locked the door to the living room where Mama and Bud were. It was cold but they were left to sleep on sofa cushions in front of a fireplace. I lay warm and comfortable in bed with Daddy. Yet I kept thinking that I ought to feel guilty for having usurped my mother's place.

I was growing up during World War II. I remember the air raids and planting a victory garden. I recall once that I was outside my house when the air raid sirens sounded. I quickly jumped into our car to wait out the warning. I felt very scared and realized that the War was real and close to home. During the War, southern boys, Black and white, joined up in vast numbers bent on reclaiming the military honor the South had lost with the defeat of the Confederacy. They were not particularly pleased to share their barracks and bunkers with Yankees and Republicans, or each other, but the military was an escape for many of them. Southern girls had little to do but plant victory gardens, sleep safely protected from an invasion, and dream of the boys who would be coming home. My dreams were also of a war hero, but it was actually me, easily vanquishing the enemy and returning in triumph to the breathlessly waiting southern belles. I would increasingly come to know that I preferred girls as my romantic interest but assumed there was nothing I could do to escape a straight life.

During this time, Mama continued her job as a cocktail waitress where she made a decent living on tips. She was attractive and vivacious and had no dearth of suitors. Since she worked a split shift from eleven in the morning until eleven at night six days a week, I seldom saw her except on Sundays. Occasionally, we would go to church together. However, sitting beside her, I knew Mama was different from the other mothers. Her dress was too fashionable, her lipstick too red, her makeup too heavy. Moreover, as far as I knew, none of the other mothers worked outside the home. They cooked and took care of the house and their children. After grandmother's death, Mama hired a series of housekeepers to take care of Bud and me. This ended when I was old enough, about twelve or thirteen, to take care of the house myself.

As our housekeepers moved away, I did the house work, looked after Bud, and prepared meals for the both of us. I detested cooking and cleaning. I still do. Even when my Mama was home, I was responsible for washing the dishes after meals. It would take me hours to finish; the water would become cold and greasy. I also had to do the grocery shopping. The store was some blocks from our house. I would return aching from carrying the paper bags of food. I did the laundry and recall hours of feeding the clean wet clothes though a rotary dryer. I did the ironing while continually in envy of Bud's appealing outdoor jobs like mowing the yard and raking leaves.

Mama was always having folks come live with us. Sometimes it would be one of her sisters, sometimes with their husbands, or another waitress from work. She was particularly close to her next oldest sister, my Aunt Verna. Once we were visiting my paternal grandfather where my Uncle John was living. He was on furlough from a psychiatric hospital. As we were leaving, Mama said "John, come to see us sometime." The next day Uncle John did, indeed, pack an old tin suitcase and walk across town to be with us.

Uncle John was with us for a few glorious weeks. He made me a gift of his baseball shoes and showed me how to clean the cleats and various other intricacies known only to the initiated. He often thought of himself as the manager of the New York Yankees – they were always winning then. He considered me a budding baseball star conveniently ignoring the fact that I was a girl. He would also sit on the front porch at a card table and write long letters to President Roosevelt. If Uncle John could direct the President as to how to run the country and win the war, I had no doubt that he could turn me into a major sports figure.

Being with Uncle John was a happy state of affairs until one evening when my cousin, Charles, who was also living with us at the time, did not come home for supper. My Mama was enormously relieved when close to midnight, Charles returned from a neighbor's house where he had been hiding. He explained that Uncle John had threatened to bash his brains in and boil them in a dishpan. Charles decided to skip the evening meal; Mama decided that Uncle John needed to go back to the hospital.

Mama was busy with her long hours at work. Perhaps this saved me since I got along so much better when she was not around. Assuming a stance of independence, I much preferred taking care of myself. Bud and I did see Daddy occasionally. We would meet him in downtown Birmingham about once a week. We walked along beside him hearing the change jingle in his pockets. He always wore a suit and tie with a hat, ever a spiffy dresser. I guess he was eager to change from his daily railroad coveralls whenever he could. He would often take us to restaurants and some afternoons to a movie theater with live stage performances including scantily dressed women. We would go through the toy departments in the various five and ten cent stores and end the visit with a trip to the drugstore. I would always have a banana split. We seldom, if ever, saw him on weekends although I remember one trip to the river with him to go fishing. I welcomed any chance to be with him and treasured our time together. I also cherished the holidays like Thanksgiving and Christmas that we spent at my grandfather's home.

In contrast to Mama, Daddy never showed emotion. This suited me fine since my hysterical mother seemed to be always chaotic and unpredictable. She was often in bed with some vague ailment or other. Daddy seemed strong and steady and I wanted to be like him. I tried never to cry, especially when I was being punished. Mama, or my grandmother, was always spanking me or my brother, usually for some transgression we did not even know we had committed. Daddy never laid a hand on us. I struggled hard to be close to him but he never overtly expressed any warmth or concern. I tried hard to gain his affection, and I still believe he loved me. Once I crawled into his lap trying to be close. He let me stay there but I had the distinct feeling that he was uncomfortable. In one memorable attempt to get to know him, I drew up my courage and asked if he believed in God. With somewhat of a dismissal, he responded that he guessed everybody did. He never let on to what he believed or what he felt. Still, I wanted to be like him. I was not aware then of his womanizing and drinking. To my Mama's credit, she never said anything to disillusion me about him.

Chapter 6
Mama's Marriages (and Divorces)

As I mentioned earlier, Mama married Daddy in the summer of 1934, after a courtship of three weeks. Daddy then struggled to find work across the Southeast. Mama stayed in Birmingham with his family or went back to Florida to her family. There was evidently considerable correspondence between them when they were away from each other. I found some of their letters after Mama died.

Once, when they were apart on December 23, 1935, after a year and a half of marriage, my Dad wrote:

"Dearest Billie,

How's the little girl making out these days? Anyway, do the best you can for the present. That's what we are doing in face of everything. No use to worry and fret, just don't do any good. Try to be your age and behave yourself.

Well, I've worked two days already (-- on the railroad --). You see, I'm working extra but I think it will be pretty good for the next week or two. Then, I hope to have a regular job. Believe me I'm trying my best and doing all I can. Eight hours is not very long . . . . Have worked hard today but I'm not so tired when I get home. I'm trying to get every day, the least will be $2.40 and that's not so bad when you consider everything. I may be able to get you a pass pretty soon so you can be going to places and seeing things without having to spend every penny for fares. Guess it will be Jan. 15 before I get my first paycheck but it will be welcome just the same. Rent here is cheap. Do you think you could manage? I think furnished rooms, three or four, are about

$10.00 for a month. . . . . I'm tickled pink with my job. Guess you are too. It may be my lucky break! Because I like it. I think it will be grand after I get a little more accustomed to it.

Xmas is going to be the same as any other Wednesday to me but maybe next one will be different. Anyway, I'm hoping to be able to make up for it. My job will be our biggest Xmas present.

I'll be thinking about you enjoying your feast. Just don't eat too much and get sick. Take good care of your health. Just be patient for a little while. Everything will be okay. Don't you think we should get some furnished rooms to begin with?

I'm glad to receive your letters every day. Keep it up. If you don't hear from me every day, think nothing of it as I'm too busy or too tired to make it every day. I try my best. Anyway, I'll send your pass when I get it. So long and good luck until next time.

With love, as ever, your friend and sweetheart and husband, Roy.

P.S. Will think about you while working Tuesday."

After nine years of marriage, my parents divorced. I have something like a diary that a high school English teacher asked me to keep. I write that:

"I came to live in South Avondale because my father and mother got a divorce and mother bought a house there. I remember the last few months we all lived together as if it were yesterday. Especially do I remember July 4, 1945, a holiday that the family spent with my grandfather. That afternoon I lay on the floor reading the funnies. I remember

that Joe Palooka burst a paper bag instead of shooting fire-
works. Then, that night we were all separated."

Although Daddy had promised Mama that someday they
would have a home for themselves, they always lived in furnished
rooms. After the divorce, determined to have her own home,
Mama, with help from her family including her sister, Verna,
bought a house in Birmingham. It was probably built in the 1920s
and was large with hardwood floors and several fireplaces. It was
on a busy street and, fortunately for me, right across from a public
park and a library. I was to spend more time in the library, happily
surrounded by books, and in the out of doors feeling more at home
than I ever did in Mama's house. She would remain in the same
home for the next twenty years. Since Daddy was usually away
working, I did not spend much time with him.

Mama was to stay single for almost ten years. She received a
little financial support from my Daddy but continually worked to
sustain us. She was a single Mom in a time when few couples
were divorced and few women were in the workforce.

Within a few years after the divorce, Daddy married Roxie, a
woman who stayed at home, cooked lovely meals, and welcomed
Bud and me into her life. As time went by, however, Roxie became unwilling to put up with Daddy's alcohol abuse and womanizing. I am not sure they ever divorced but they lived apart for
many years. Daddy always had a woman in his life including
someone strange to us who had evidently been with him shortly
before his death. She came to his funeral service and sat silently
in the rear. Daddy worked on the railroad all of his life. He died
of a heart attack in 1974 just two weeks before he was to retire.

Mama dated many different men but was particularly close
with our next-door neighbor, Clarence Simmons. He worked for
the Ford dealership repairing cars. In the summer of 1954, my

Mom wrote me a letter. (I had left home on the day after my high school graduation). She asked if Clarence had called me and filled her letter with some small comments or another. She then briefly wrote, "as soon as Clarence gets his vacation, we are getting married." This was to be the week that I entered college. She had spent ten years with my brother and me – and the series of men she dated – but was now to return to the safety of marriage and having a man on her arm.

Ten years later, I received a letter from Clarence:

"Yes, Bonnie, I signed the divorce papers for Billie. I didn't want it this way but she did. Wish I had had knowledge enough to have prevented it for I love Billie and guess I always will. But, she told me that she didn't love me anymore, didn't want to live with me anymore, was unhappy and wanted a divorce, also asked me to move out, in fact she moved what few things I had to an apartment while I was at work. So, I didn't see that I had any choice but to sign the papers. She was very sweet about it, worked herself until she almost dropped. She was not mad at me; we had no cross words. She said that she was going to get a divorce and there was nothing I could do to prevent it.

Bonnie, I regret very much that his has happened but I want you to know that I will always have the greatest respect for your mother. I think she is a very sweet girl and I will always be grateful for the many nice and thoughtful deeds she has done for me over the past 18 years of love and friendship. I really miss her. I hope she finds the most happiness anyone could have.

Bonnie, if you are over in Birmingham, please come by. I would be just happy to see you. And, if I ever get to Atlanta and have any time, you may just have company.

Thanks for the invitation.
  Love and goodnight,
  C.V. Simmons"

I continued to see Clarence, although I am not sure Mama did. I sent him Father's Day cards and visited him every time I was back in Birmingham. He was always glad to see me. He lived alone until his death at age 100.

After the divorce from Clarence, Mama moved back to Florida and settled on a piece of land close to the old home place. She decided to build a house, but she actually bought a trailer and placed it on the bank of the river swamp. Bill Roemer, a widower, came by to help her with the septic system. He worked at the local paper mill, but was much respected in the community and served on the school board. They married within the year.

Another ten years passed. By this time I was living in Massachusetts but would go back to visit my old home in Atlanta as often as I could. I had sold the house to a close friend, Sylvia, and would usually stay there when I was back in Atlanta. On one of these visits, Sylvia came into my bedroom about 6:30 in the morning. She said your mother's on the phone. I quickly took the call fully expecting some dire emergency. Mama calmly announced, "Oh, I thought I might find you here." She went on to say that she was traveling through Atlanta to visit my brother, Bud, in South Carolina. She was with Uncle Jennings in his pickup truck and said she had some furniture to deliver to Bud (she did not bring me anything). In addition, Uncle Jennings was to have some dental work. Bud, being a dentist, was always providing pro bono services to family members.

I asked Mama to stop by. She came and sat on a sofa in the living room. Settled with a cup of coffee, she talked briefly and then went on to say, almost as an afterthought, that she was leaving her third husband, Bill. Bill, as it turned out, had been away from their home visiting his son who was in the hospital in another town with a broken arm. Mama looked somewhat rueful and said perhaps she should have left him a note. She also remarked that she was not sure she had put the cat out.

I was surprised, but accepted the news in my usual stoic manner. Looking back on my childhood, I realized that Mama forever trailed uncertainty and unpredictability in her wake. I gave up trying to understand her but would steel myself for surprise, mostly unpleasant, and try to maintain a stoicism I did not really feel. My responses were stony silence. I tried to protect myself from her unexpected whims and retreated into my own sullen self. I built a world of books and fantasies to keep me from her reach. I never felt secure or safe but determined that I would have to be independent and take care of myself. Given that, I am surprised that I have been able to maintain warm and sustained personal relationships in my adult life; I never leave old friends. Perhaps I learned my fierce loyalty in contrast to the shallow model of my Mama.

Within a very few months after leaving Bill, or perhaps earlier – this would have been in the mid to late 1990s – Mama met Red Albright. He was good looking, about her age, and seemed to enjoy being with her. They were together for about 10 years, Mama's usual tenure for a marriage, when she decided they should actually get married. The wedding did not come off quite as planned. Mama and Red were at my home in Belchertown, Massachusetts when she decided that it was time for the wedding. The minister was to be a faculty friend who had some license or recognition from the Universal Life Church.

We invited a number of friends, ordered a cake and champagne, and gathered up whatever glasses we had. We were prepared to celebrate the happy event in the late afternoon of a beautiful day (both spouses were in their late 70s, early 80s). As I lived on a lake, early in the afternoon Red decided to go fishing. However, he could not find a hook for the fishing line. He kept pestering my mother as to where it might be. She kept telling him to go to the garage and look through the fishing tackle box. Red, perhaps in the early stages of Alzheimer's, was not able to find a hook and kept asking over and over again where it could be. Exasperated, Mama responded to his inquiries by calling off the wedding.

So, here we were with cake, champagne, guests, and a pseudo minister expected any moment. Although not usually able to rise to crises, in this emergency Mama decided to change the wedding event into a birthday party. When they arrived, folks seemed a bit confused but joined in the newly acclaimed celebration with considerable enthusiasm. A good time was had by all, including Red, although he did seem a bit put out that he never found a fishhook.

Mama and Red went back to Florida where they had been living. Red became even more seriously cognitively challenged and went into a nursing home. Mama moved to South Carolina to be close to my brother but she, too, began to have signs of encroaching Alzheimer's. Having outlived her three husbands and Red, she moved for the last time to enter a nursing home close to me. She died a few months later at age eighty-four.

Chapter 7

Growing Up in the Steel City

Although our home was Birmingham, life there never felt as comfortable to me as Florida. I was no longer one among many, but rather enmeshed with an unpredictable mother, an absent father, and a brother who enjoyed the male prerogatives I always craved. Everyone treated me like the girl I never wanted to be. I was also growing up in one of the most segregated and prejudiced cities in the country.

Aside from race, Birmingham was not particularly diverse. The city was young, having been established after the Civil War as a railway hub and a site where iron, coal and limestone were all found proximate to each other.

Men, mostly of English, Irish, Scottish and Welsh descent, rushed to the city to find jobs in the nearby mines and the steel mills. Birmingham was a place where cheap, non-unionized and African-American labor could be employed, giving it a competitive advantage over industrial cities in the Midwest and Northeast. Black men, especially, had the most menial and lowest paying jobs. Except for the mill owners and managers who lived in lovely communities a bit south of the city, Birmingham was a rough and rowdy working class town.

Businesses, churches, parks, public accommodations, restaurants, and schools, were strictly segregated. Seating was separate on the city buses and public drinking fountains were reserved for either whites or Colored. Once, in a department store I mistakenly drank from the Colored water fountain. When I realized what I had done, I looked around fearfully waiting for some reprimand. I was enormously relieved when I found that no one had seen me.

While I was growing up, Birmingham did not have a museum,

a ballet company, an opera company, live theater or art museums as it does now. Our grandest culture was a movie theater that had a large organ, which emerged from the floor at special times before the movie. There also was an auditorium where Daddy occasionally took Bud and me to wrestling matches. Nor did the city attract enclaves of recent ethnic immigrants who might have brought their own diverse cultures. I did come to have a Greek friend, but was never invited to visit her home.

My elementary school was located on a boundary between working class (my neighborhood) and more affluent families. The student body was all white. There were no Black students, of course, but nor were there any Latino or Asian or any other non-Western European students.

Probably a quarter of the students in my elementary school class were Jewish. Although I was never invited to their homes, I came to know them well and several were close friends. I was pleased to know that their families were people of some distinction. They owned businesses in downtown Birmingham. I was particularly proud to go into their department stores and shop, and occasionally I would meet one of the fathers of a classmate. My impression was that the Jewish families were well to do and I knew few folks like that. The only professional person in my neighborhood I ever saw, and never met, was a doctor in my church. Being raised a staunch Southern Baptist, I was concerned that my Jewish friends did not believe in Jesus Christ as their personal savior. I was afraid that they were all going to hell.

The other of my elementary classmates were Protestant. To my knowledge, no one was Catholic. I met my first Catholic when I was in high school and Margaret Malcolm became my best friend. I remember being in the gym locker room, looking across at her while she was dressing, thinking that even as a Catholic, she looked altogether normal. I was perturbed, however, because

I thought Catholics were damned by having to pray to the Pope and the Virgin Mary, while I had a direct link to Jesus.

Although I did not know it then, this may have been one of the first times that seeing friends dressing piqued my sexual interest in girls. I had huge crushes on Margaret and another friend, Meg. I had seen Meg in her slip and my vivid memories of her and Margaret dressing likely marked my budding sexuality.

During this time, I was enormously curious about homosexuality. I did everything I could to educate myself about it. I kept looking around to see if I could identify a homosexual. As far as I know, except for the two women who lived together next door, I grew up in a heterosexual and ordinary community. Still, I came to know a few benignly eccentric folks, who could have been gay or lesbian. In the 1940s and 50s, however, the term lesbian was reserved for a minor Greek poet and none of us were reading the classics.

I knew not one Black person although I lived surrounded by Black communities. One hot, humid summer day, I was about ten years old riding my bicycle on a sidewalk close to home. Rounding the corner, I came face to face with an African-American girl about my age also on a bicycle. I stared at her and she stared back. Until that time, I do not think I had ever been close to a Black child. I had seen many Black people but never up close. I was immediately curious about her life and wondered how similar or different we might be from each other. I wondered if she was thinking the same. We looked at each other for a moment and then went our separate ways.

The next individual Black person I saw, maybe a couple of years later, was a woman who came to our door. I do not recall what she was there for, but I talked to her and said, "Yes, ma'am." Later Mama told me that I should not say "ma'am" or "sir" to a Black person. I remember thinking there was something not quite right about this. I was confused. I had always been taught to say "sir" and "ma'am" to grownups and I did not understand this correction. Why was it all right to call white adults "ma'am" or "sir" but not Blacks? Why race should make a difference was beyond me. When I was growing up, I did not think much about our mixed culture. Segregation was a given and not discussed. I knew of the Black neighborhoods and that a large number of Black people lived in Birmingham. I also knew of a Black family who lived next door to my maternal grandparents in Dalkeith. One of the adult women had been a wet nurse to my mother. I do not recall being prejudiced or feeling animosity toward Blacks. I suspect that from an early age I saw myself somewhat connected to them. Like them, I was disadvantaged. While they may have been judged by the color of their skin, I felt equally judged as inferior by being poor, by being a girl, and by being gender non-conforming. Like them, I was an outsider to the majority world.

In school, in my Alabama History class, (we never had world history or United States history), I was inundated with tales of how the Union Army stooped below the bounds of recognized military warfare to win what we called the War of Northern Aggression.

We southerners were a defeated people. Although to my knowledge, I had never met one, my overriding disdain was for Yankees – anyone American not from the Deep South. Growing up I continued to fight the Civil War with slogans of "The South will rise again" and "Save your confederate money."

I was taught that ours had been the only part of this country, aside from Indian lands, that had ever been occupied by foreign (to us) troops. The savagery of the war had not only decimated our men but also attacked the livelihood of our southern citizens by burning crops in the field and our very homes and buildings.

Like other southern children, I was taught of the destruction of our economy. Reconstruction brought Carpetbaggers, Scalawags and Black politicians. Seventy five years after the War, I grew up as if these events had only happened yesterday. I saw all around me the remnants of a defeated nation. What I did not see were the effects of segregation and Jim Crow laws.

Proud to be a Southerner, I cheered Strom Thurman in 1947 when he organized the Dixiecrats and marched out of the Democratic Convention with southern delegates in support of state's rights. After all, although we had lost a war over this issue, or so I had been taught, wasn't there a possibility we would have another chance to defend our stance? Of course, at the ripe old age of 11, I had no idea that the term, states' rights, was code for segregation.

Looking back, I realize that I lived in a truly segregated bubble. I had come to know some Jewish children but no minorities and no one whose forbearers had come from non-Western countries. I knew no Yankees, Republicans, or gay people and now surprise myself that I eventually came to know people of diverse cultures whom I welcome into my life.

Chapter 8
Tomboy or Transgender?

There was a folk tale I had heard of that if you could kiss your elbow you would turn into the opposite sex. I was not quite convinced this was true, but I almost broke my arm trying. From an early age, I knew that I would have preferred to be a boy. Conventional notions of feminine behavior were foreign to me and even frightening. My only experience of female role models had been my grandmother, Mama, and my aunts. They worked hard, bore the responsibility of children, and seemed to have little fun. Men, on the other hand, had the power of making the major decisions in the family, worked outside the home, and enjoyed a freedom from everyday household chores. They went fishing, hunting, to ball games and enjoyed their free time. No wonder I preferred male prerogatives.

Once, when Mama was having her hair done at the beauty parlor down the street, I received a telephone message that needed to be delivered to her. I stood at the door to the shop in absolute panic. All courage left me when I was faced with the scent of shampoo and the warm, moist heat of the hair dryers in this women's sanctuary. I dashed in, delivered the message, and frantically escaped back into the fresh air. I was frightened, perhaps, by the glimpse of my future as a grown-up woman. It would be years before I would feel comfortable in a beauty parlor. I was in my forties before I had a massage.

Although we could hardly afford it, Mama kept up with the latest fashion and dressed well. She was always carefully made up and my brother says he still remembers the scent of her perfume as she walked through a room. Once, she asked me if the powder on her face was caked. How would I know? I did not have a clue. I could easily calibrate the ratio of oil to gas for a two-cycle engine, but I had no idea of how to apply powder and lipstick, nor did I want to learn. Still, I looked knowingly at her and remarked that I thought she looked fine.

When I was growing up as a kid we never took vacations but, occasionally on Sundays and holidays, we would visit my paternal grandfather, friends of Mama's, or distant cousins who lived in Birmingham. Bud and I were always well dressed, respectful of our elders, and sat quietly through the visits. We were with Mama as nothing more than tag along children.

For as long as I can recall, Mama was always and continually involved with men. She was attractive and sociable and never without a date. Many of the men were in her life for long periods of time. I came to know them well and they always treated Bud and me kindly. On Sundays, when Mama was off from work, we might drive out to the river. Mama and her date would hang out at the local bar, while Bud and I would play in the nearby water.

In my growing up days, being boyish in all things, I longed to wear boy's clothes. I remember with great delight one of the most precious gifts I ever received as a child. One of the recreation directors in the park across the street gave me a shirt that may have been a boy's shirt. It was a simple short-sleeved yellow cotton shirt and I do not know why she gave it to me. I loved it. Maybe because it was a gift from someone who noticed me or because there was delight for me in wearing a boy's shirt. Either way, I wore it everywhere.

Back then, cross dressers were called transsexuals and the term transgender was well into the future. As times have changed and more and more people are transitioning, I realize that I might have been a transgender child. I wanted to be a boy and would sometimes stand in front of a mirror and flex my biceps. My life was all boyish but, at that time, no one was considering the possibility of a sex change. I was simply a tomboy.

Mama kept insisting that I be more feminine. She wanted me to bathe and insisted that I wash my hair. She and I would almost always get into a fight when she tried to wash my hair. I hated anyone to touch my hair and dreaded the times when it had to be washed. Mama wanted to curl it, but I adamantly refused. I begged for short hair, but it was not to be. The best I could do was talk her into pigtails. We argued about my hair as long as I can remember.

No doubt, my masculine nature was a major problem for my ultra-feminine Mama. While she was doing her best to raise me as a socialized girl child, I insisted on pursuing boyish activities, rebelling at feminine clothes and household chores. She tried in vain to dress me in frilly dresses, a struggle that succeeded only when I had to wear evening dresses for some best-forgotten piano recitals. Boys had all the fun and would not be caught dead in a dress, an attitude I fully endorsed. While I could not change my physical sex, I could at least behave and think like a boy and pretend that I was one. Boys were my preferred playmates, colleagues in adventure, and best friends. Girls were rather weak, exotic creatures who needed to be pampered and protected. I always thought I should take care of them.

My impression of males was that if they even had feelings, they never expressed them. I tried to emulate them. I determined that I would never admit to or recognize having any feelings and certainly not let other people know of them. I never talked about my innermost thoughts unless they fell in the expected male-type conversations. I easily fell into discussions about heavyweight boxing, car racing, and major league baseball. I knew the batting average of every player and the earned run stats for each pitcher on our beloved Birmingham Barons minor league baseball team. I could hold forth indefinitely on the horsepower, styling, and fuel requirements of any late model car. Falling back on my Florida adventures, I could talk endlessly about the relative merits of shotguns versus rifles for killing almost any creature. I always knew the perfect lure and bait for fishing.

I played with the neighborhood children much preferring the boys. We had no television so after school, during the long afternoons, we children would play around the neighborhood. I always tried to be the leader. Living across from the park, I engaged in the summer recreational activities and the supervised games. I often won prizes for activities like horseshoes and jump rope. Once my dog, Archibald, won first prize in a pet show for having the "queerest" name. He won second prize for being the ugliest dog. I was a little hurt, but he was truly a mongrel, like all of the dogs that I had as a child. I do not know where they came from but there was a series of dogs to which I gave exotic names like Hornbuckle and Jeremiah. I also had three snakes to whom I gave Biblical names, Shadrach, Meshach, and Abednego. My mother would usually give the dogs away saying they would be happier on some farm that she had found. I really do not know where they went.

As soon as I was grown and able, I bought my first dog, a German shepherd that I named Jefferson Davis. Having just moved north, I could not resist some remembrance of my southern home. I have always had a dog, and sometimes cats. They have brought me great joy. As an adult, I bred and showed dogs, starting with German shepherds and then Labrador Retrievers.

In the public park across from my home, I was able to join some of the boys' teams and at one proud moment was named center on the all-boys (weighing no more than 90 pounds) YMCA football team. Needless to say, Mama did not share my excitement. In her continued, mostly unsuccessful attempts to feminize me, she determined that I should no longer play with the boys.

No more pickup games, no more long afternoons in the park hanging out with the guys.

Actually, she would have been thrilled if I "played" with boys the way most girls did – the shy giggles, the flirting, and the flattery. My style of play was the rough-and-tumble touching of young males still more interested in physical prowess than sexual innuendo.

Unable to go to the park, I sat on the steps of our front porch gazing across to the lost fields, a familiar but distant shore to which I could not return. Hurt and helpless, all my boyish bravado vanished. I sobbed like the sissy girl Mama always wanted me to be.

Being an enterprising youngster, when I was about fifteen or so, I simply wandered from the football fields to the softball diamonds. I was in luck. I found a mostly lesbian softball team. No doubt, Mama would have joyfully reconsidered her decision for me to quit playing with boys if she had known that I was going to be going to their practices and games. I had kept statistics on the games played by our Birmingham Barons, a minor league baseball team. It was an easy step for me to become the scorekeeper for the team. I sat on the bench with the players and became their batgirl. I was never old enough or good enough to actually play in their games, but occasionally they let me bat or play in the field during their practices.

Most of these women worked in the mills, dressed in men's clothes, and kept a ring of keys on their belts. They also were as good at brawling as they were at playing ball. I learned from them that you could really hurt someone if you spread keys between your fingers and used them to cut the other person.

After one game, we found that the opposing team had slashed the tires on the cars of some of our players. We followed them to a bar, where they were drinking beer and having supper, and invited them out into the parking lot. One woman from the other team and one of our team members began to fight. Our first baseman, keys between fingers, circled the fighting duo and insisted that no one else join in. Actually, I doubt that this would have prevented what was rapidly about to turn into a brawl for everyone. I was secretly hoping it would continue and expand. I wanted to jump in. I was so proud of my team. Here were strong, proud women asserting their power, refusing to back down, and responding fiercely to an insult to their integrity. Then, we heard the approaching sirens of the police. Our team quickly left the scene leaving the opposing team, which was trying to retrieve belongings from inside the bar, to face the authorities.

I was the team groupie for several years. I realize now that these women were lesbians, but I did not know that then. I simply did not know that there were lesbians in the world.

The players never once mentioned anything sexual or intimated that they were gay. They never touched each other in my presence or looked to be other than friends. No doubt, I was questioning, but these women gave me no evidence of being gay nor did they ever make a suggestive move on me.

Homosexuality was a taboo topic, a perversion. No one wanted to be known as outing a vulnerable teenager to a life of sin and suffering. I simply gloried in having found a place where a group of women accepted me as I was and let me be a part of their softball life. I was around people I cherished; dare say loved, where women dressed as they pleased and found joy in their play and in each other.

They laughed a lot and tousled my hair. The first baseman gave me a baseball cap with the team emblem on it. I wore it everywhere except to bed. I still have it packed away with the memories of strong women, who by opening their hearts to me opened mine. Throughout my adulthood, softball was to remain a treasured sport and wherever I was, I tried to find a team to join.

Although I enjoyed my play with the neighborhood kids, I also pursued solitary activities. We did not have books in the house, nor did my family subscribe to a daily paper. I did read my Daddy's union newspaper when I was visiting him. I was an avid reader and spent long hours with books from the library across the street. I preferred adventure stories, written primarily for boys, until Nancy Drew came along. Generally, my tastes were eclectic.

Mama decided some of the books I checked out were too advanced for me. She went to the librarian and asked that she limit my book choices. The librarian agreed to monitor the books I checked out, but I never really knew what she held back. I remember the name of the book that Mama objected to. It was Half a Hemisphere; I do not remember what it was about. I should go back and look at it again. I always wondered why Mama talked to the librarian. Maybe she was trying to protect me in some way, or perhaps she did not want me to outdo her intellectually or otherwise. There would be other times later that she would also sabotage my academic efforts.

I am grateful that although she did everything to feminize me, Mama did allow me some boys' toys, like a cap gun and an erector set. I also had a collection of radio parts and built my own crystal radio. In addition, there was my beloved chemistry set. I managed to eke out space under our back porch to spread out the chemicals and the various apparatus. I learned to blow glass and mix up special concoctions. My biggest adventure was discovering that the chemical set had enough ingredients that I could mix a potent brew to explode as flare bombs in the back yard. A budding female uni-bomber, I was rapidly becoming a public menace.

My interests in science led me to give up my thoughts of becoming a missionary. I gave up looking to the heavens for God and decided to become an astrophysicist, exploring the planets instead of people's souls. If astronauts had been more of a reality then, rather than a science fiction fantasy, they would have been my heroes.

I yearned for a life beyond the sludge of the swamps and the soot of the steel mills. I pictured myself a medical scientist in a clean white lab coat finding a cure for cancer or an astronomer discovering a new star. Yet, I knew in my heart that the closest I would get to the stars was in a sports arena.

Acting like a boy meant never engaging in displays of physical affection or being weak. There were no hugs or kisses in my family. Although my outdoor adventures would occasionally lead to scrapes and bruises, I refused to admit pain.

One summer, when I was about twelve, I fell and cut my palm on some cinders. I never mentioned the swelling or the red marks that were running up my arm. In my sleep, however, I rolled over on my hand and cried out. Mama heard me and came into my room to see what was wrong. I showed her my hand. The next morning she took me to the doctor. He lanced it and said I should immediately go to the hospital. Turned out I loved being in the hospital.

I was there for a week with my infected hand. The summer heat was unbearable as there was no air conditioning in those days. My room was on a first floor hall where the nurses had to pass through to go to their residence. One nurse would stop by late at night as she was going off duty and rub my back with alcohol to cool me off.

I began to think there must be something to this "touching" business and wanted more. Her back rubs reminded me of the one other time that I recall the warmth of being positively touched.

I was also about twelve having a sleep over with a girlfriend. Before we went to sleep, we turned toward each other and clasped hands. In all of my young life, these are the only times I remember being touched by another with affection.

When the doctors asked me if I was ready to go home, I said no, and they let me stay an extra day. It is a wonder I didn't become a chronic hypochondriac. However, that would have made me more like Mama, who was always coming down with vague aches and pains and mysterious illnesses. I had to be the strong, healthy one.

All of the other touching I knew was from being physically punished. I did not usually understand why I was being hit or switched.

Once Mama discovered me climbing on the top of the roof of our house. I was probably about thirty or forty feet in the air. She called me down and spanked me in front of my friends, an added humiliation. I began to plan strategies to avoid her. On Sundays, the only day that she was not working, I would spend as much time in church as I could. People in the congregation must have admired my devotion, completely unaware that church was an escape for me.

I began to try to avoid misbehaving in any way. I became rule bound and obsessive about how to avoid mistakes. I was ever vigilant about being discovered in some aberrant behavior. Knowing that Mama was unpredictable, I would try to merge into the background and do anything I could to help sooth her behavior. I felt responsible for her and the need to protect her from herself. By protecting her, I could protect myself.

Chapter 9

A Budding Jock

My Uncle Bill put up a basketball goal in our back yard. During my growing up years, I spent many hours tossing a ball toward the hoop, always by myself. I don't know why I didn't invite other kids to join me, but I rather enjoyed working on my shots without an audience. I would dream of sinking the winning basket in a championship game, this in spite of the reality that athletics were a male prerogative. Girls were not welcomed nor allowed in organized team sports such as Little League. I did play pickup games, almost always with boys. I would not play on any organized team until my late teens.

I suspected that when I was 18 or so I would join the military like my cousins and other poor southerners, Black and white. Girls were more likely to be military wives than soldiers. I could not envision this as my path to the world I had read about in books on philosophy, poetry and science. Yet, higher education was a foreign concept to me. I did not know anyone who had ever gone to college, except schoolteachers. While never giving up the dream of becoming a teacher, which began when I started school, I thought perhaps I would become a professional athlete.

I would spend hours in our neighbor's driveway next to our house hitting a tennis ball against the wall. One magic day, a neighbor, Eunice Foster, came bicycling by, stopped, and asked if I wanted her to teach me tennis in the park across the street. A single woman in her forties or fifties, I realize now that she may have been a lesbian. Such a concept was well beyond me at that time and certainly, she never evidenced any suggestion of the possibility of same sex attraction. I was blessed that she became my mentor. I treasure the gift of tennis that she gave me. The sport began an adventure that was to lead me well beyond the driveway. Not only did Ms. Foster teach me tennis, she also introduced me to other players and the opportunity to compete in some public parks tournaments. I began to win and was invited to play at the Birmingham Country Club. Mama, having heard me practicing the piano for years, knew immediately that tennis was a better investment. In one of the few incidences where my desires and Mama's support coalesced, she paid for lessons from the club pro. Tennis is a rather elite sport. It is interesting that for a kid like me, from a working class background, tennis would open doors that I could never have imagined. I joined a Junior Wightman Cup team for girls that involved traveling and playing tournaments. MacGregor, a major tennis business, sponsored me and gave me free racquets. I traveled in rare company playing competitive tennis. In 1953, when I was fifteen, I won the Doubles title for the state of Alabama. I was nationally ranked in the under 16-age class. I was also playing on my high school boys' tennis team. My dreams shifted and I wanted to pursue a career in professional tennis. I was especially emboldened when another kid from the South, Althea Gibson, became the first Black woman to win at Wimbledon.

Tennis took me to places very different from my neighborhood and to people very different from my neighbors. It was, indeed, a culture clash. I felt very self-conscious and afraid of making mistakes.

A tennis friend invited me to lunch at her home on the county club side of town. I walked through the door and saw beautiful wallpaper and oriental carpets on the floor. Her mother had prepared the meal. We ate in a lovely dining room. It was the most beautiful house I had ever been in.

All of a sudden, I realized how shabby Mama's home was compared to those of the rich. I was also aware that my adult male neighbors, bus drivers and bakers, were different from the fathers of my new tennis friends who were doctors, lawyers and business executives. Aside from my hospital experience and the physicians in the public health clinics we visited, I had never met other professionals such as attorneys or business folks, all of whom would have been men at that time. Needless to say, I never envisioned myself entering a professional career, although I dreamed of becoming something more than a cocktail waitress like Mama.

My new adventures across town whetted my curiosity about other people's families. I saw that other families, even in our working class neighborhood, usually had meals together, at least breakfast and dinner.

I would often wander over to a neighbor's house, Bud in tow, where we were invariably asked to stay for supper. Southerners always want to feed you. Bud and I gave our neighbors the opportunity to bring new meaning to the word hospitality. I was also intrigued by the fact that married couples usually stayed together; mothers were at home and cooked. Fathers worked outside the home, but were present for dinner.

Two women lived together next door to us, so I grew up thinking that was not entirely unusual. I had a neighbor with epilepsy who, whether safe or not, drove me to tennis and I learned of his condition.

During my growing up days, Bud, four years younger, was an ever-constant presence. I do not remember much about our relationship. We did play some board games together. I beat him regularly in Monopoly and would at times beat him literally for some perceived fault. Physical competition was clear to me. I understood the dictates of brute strength. I knew the thrill of contact and the benefits of cease-fire. However, the long-term physical abuse that I visited on Bud ended one day when he flexed his muscles and slammed me through an open door. No parental interference, no psychotherapy or mediation, just immediate conflict resolution and simple justice through one well-placed punch.

Bud was a good athlete, learning to play tennis at an early age. This would hold him in good stead. He played well enough to eventually secure a full tennis scholarship to college, where all of his expenses were paid.

Bud also had the privilege, denied to girls at that time, of playing on a local Little League baseball team. He was a left-handed pitcher who played through such a successful season that the team was invited to the national championships in Williamsport, Pennsylvania. The team won the national title and returned triumphantly to Birmingham.

Although I do not recall Mama attending my tennis matches, she did accompany Bud and the team to Pennsylvania. As always, he was the preferred child simply for being male. Aside from constantly fighting, Bud and I had little to do with each other. We were not in contact for many years after I went off to college.

Chapter 10

High School Days

On the first day of high school, September 1950, I went by myself to catch a public bus to ride across town. I was not quite sure of where I was going and fearful of what awaited. The school was on a busy street in a crowded neighborhood with about two thousand students, all white. I think it was the largest in the city of Birmingham.

I was lost from the start, knowing almost no one and in no classes with the kids from my old school. Later I would make a few new friends, but mostly I was isolated and lonely. I never saw a guidance counselor, although I suppose the school had them. I was left on my own to decide what classes to take.

During the first couple of years of high school, I had a job in the library across the street from our home. As always, I loved being in the world of books. I had a chance to see all of the new ones coming in and wrapped them in cellophane to keep them clean. I was responsible for reshelving the returned books. Eleanor Starnes, the rather prim and proper librarian, kept a strict, do not disturb, atmosphere in the library.

One summer she was away and two sisters took her place. They were much more lenient, even noisy at times. I felt torn in my loyalty to Ms. Starnes, but pleasantly surprised by the more relaxed atmosphere. Perhaps this was the time that I first began to question whether I would make my living as an athlete. I had always enjoyed reading and the world of books and, as was true when I was younger, I thought I might become a librarian. Nevertheless, mainly I remained faithful to my dream of becoming a teacher.

The library job was my first paying one and I dutifully gave my wages to Mama. In what was a useless effort to gain her affection, I would save money and buy her expensive gifts. It never occurred to me to use the money for myself. Mama had bound me to her in every way including financially. I wanted to please her and take care of her. Yet, I was increasingly becoming independent and began to think more about myself as separate from her. Do folks really enjoy being in high school? I never did. My elementary school was on the border of two neighborhoods so that students who graduated went to one of two high schools. My high school was in a working class community where few of the graduates went to college. The other was academically superior with all sorts of help for college preparation. I lost many friends and many opportunities to that school.

Being in elementary school and at the library had always been a pleasant experience for me. However, I was lost in high school and never enjoyed it, except when I was involved in sports. Although still dreaming of being a teacher, I considered several other occupations such as becoming a professional athlete or a librarian.

I knew that to prepare for college, I would have to complete some of the most demanding courses. I took Latin with a vague notion that it would prepare me to be a doctor since it was the basis of some of the language of medicine. I did not do well, but felt I needed to learn a language and turned to French. I enjoyed my science courses and did well in math, although I never took algebra or calculus. I tried to help with audiovisual equipment in some of my classes. The teachers began to depend on me to run films, especially my household physics teacher. He, too, fondled me sexually and, as usual, I never told anyone. When I graduated from high school, he gave me a matched luggage set which I still have. Now that would immediately send up signals about an inappropriate relationship, but Mama did not seem to notice.

As part of my efforts at fitting in, I dated boys from my high school. They were all working class with no plans to go to college. We did the usual high school dating, kissing and fondling each other although we never "went all the way," as intercourse was described in those days.

I enjoyed the typical dates that meant cruising the streets, frequenting the local dairy bars, and going to drive in movies. None of us drank alcohol and this was well before drugs.

Perhaps the time I enjoyed the most with these boys, however, was helping them work on their cars. I also played tennis with one boy I was seeing. He said I was "pretty good" for a girl. Still being involved in church activities, I would sometime accompany him to the local jails. We would sing hymns and read the Bible while trying to convert the inmates.

Some of the boys I dated would push for more sexual intimacy. I always resisted, first because I thought sex was a sin. Perhaps more importantly, I simply was not interested.

I had begun to realize that I had feelings toward girls. These were, however, primarily emotional. It did not occur to me that one might enjoy sexual relationships with other girls. This would come later as I emerged into young adulthood. In the meantime, I enjoyed deep friendships with my close girlfriends, never believing that our relationships could be any different.

In high school, physical education – gym – was my favorite class but I also enjoyed science and English. I was a good athlete. I worked hard to impress my teachers, particularly the student teachers. I had crushes on several of them and wanted to spend time with them. Taking lots of physical education allowed me that. My senior year, I was named best female athlete in the school.

I continued to involve myself in sports, both in and outside of school. There were no team sports for girls although I did play on the high school boys' tennis team.

In order to accompany the football team, I tried out for cheerleader. I did not have the grace and style to make the cut. Obviously, I would have preferred to try out for the football team. I was deeply hurt to be rejected but never admitted it.

Sports and athletics were my salvation for having led me to my high school gym teacher. Louise Pope was likely in her forties or early fifties and had been teaching at the high school for many years. I never really found out much about her personal life. She seemed happily married. Somehow, I learned that although she and her husband had wanted to have children, she had suffered a number of miscarriages and was childless. Maybe I was the daughter she never had. Maybe she was the mother I always wanted. Whatever the reasons, she became my mentor and would lead me to college.

Mrs. Pope talked to me about my classes and asked about my grades. When I was supposed to take my report card home and have it signed by a parent, I simply gave it to her and she signed it. When I narrowly missed being tapped for a national honor society, she angrily stormed into the principal's office to find out why. No one had ever stood up for me like that before.

Mrs. Pope, who lived not too far from me, would occasionally drive me to school and back. Those were the days when one had to pay household bills at the utility offices. Sometimes, she would let me go with her. Once, on one of our trips, she looked over at me and remarked that when she was my age she also liked to wear boyish clothes. But, she suggested that I might want to dress a little more feminine.

I listened carefully. I knew she was trying to offer me advice in a kind way; I welcomed her comments. Her concern was one of the first times that someone had tried to explain something to me with sensitivity and kindness. Goodness knows I needed advice and socializing. I tried to follow her advice and picked out some more feminine clothes to wear. I understood that she was trying to be helpful and I wanted to please her.

One piece of advice was especially important and changed my life. I was thinking that after high school, I would take up a career in professional tennis and not go to college. Mrs. Pope, on hearing of my thoughts, immediately remarked that I should give up that idea and put college first. She talked of a former student who had become a golf pro and could not make a living, a situation she did not want for me. She simply insisted that I go to college.

Others that had a strong influence during my high school years were the student physical education teachers. They all came from a small Baptist college in the community. I began to think about going there when I graduated and majoring in physical education. One student teacher, in particular, took an interest in me and let me go with her to some Red Cross Life Saving classes at the local YWCA. I hardly knew how to swim but I was certified as having completed the courses. My life saving badge was to land me a job when I eventually did get to college.

Mama had announced that while my Grandfather Strickland had promised to assist me financially in going to college, he changed his mind. I remember exactly where I was, in my bedroom, and the despair I felt when she told me this. My hopes were dashed. It appeared that like my peers, I would graduate from high school, marry, and start a family.

Once again, Mrs. Pope came to my rescue. She sent me to her old college, Alabama College, only slightly more creative than its name, to compete for scholarships. I received a Linley Heflin scholarship of $250. I was also promised a job working in the dining hall. The combined monies would enable me to pay the full cost, $536 per year, of attending the school. This included tuition, fees, room and board, laundry and health care.

A women's philanthropic group in Birmingham bestowed the Linley Heflin Scholarship to needy girls. I was surprised and thrilled to receive the money. Begun during the First World War, the first women rolled bandages and helped provide supplies for the troops. Some fifteen years after my graduation from college, when I had moved to Massachusetts, I received a call from a Linley Heflin member. She asked if I would return to Birmingham and give a talk at one of their luncheons. I immediately said yes, willing to do anything to show my appreciation for my early college support.

We agreed on the date. I then asked how many would be attending the luncheon. The woman responded, 1700. Turns out this was their annual fundraising event, complete with a fashion show featuring nationally known fashion designers. Being a professor, I suspected that I would have little trouble speaking, but what was I going to wear?

Mrs. Pope and I remained in contact for many, many years throughout my college and graduate school days as well as during my professional career. I would visit her at her home and thank her for being interested in and caring for me. She would say she was proud of me. I delighted in our relationship.

Once, after about a year of not hearing from her, I went to her home, knocked on the door, and she did not appear. I became somewhat frantic, but could not find any neighbors to tell me of her whereabouts. I suspected that she had moved or gone to a nursing home, but I had no way to contact her.

When I did not receive a Christmas card from her that year, I knew she was gone from me. I still think of her often realizing with great sadness that I never had a chance to say goodbye. She changed my life, not only in regard to getting me into college and guiding my career, but also emotionally in terms of her respect for me. I was beginning to feel that I might be able to make something of myself. Without judgment, she let me be who I was and because of her, I started to feel good about myself and the decisions I was making.

As I mentioned, I played on the boys' tennis team. The coach of the team had likely talked to Mrs. Pope. Somehow, he knew I was good at tennis and better than some of the boys on his team. He welcomed me and treated me as a full team member. The boys, as well, allowed as if I was one of them. We traveled to play other high school teams and delighted in our wins. I regularly beat the opposing fellows, who were humiliated at losing to a girl.

I had several close girlfriends, mostly from the church, although they were not necessarily a good influence. They would occasionally skip school and ask me to join them. Somehow, Mrs. Pope found out about their misadventures and warned me to behave myself. I never joined them in skipping school, but I was particularly drawn to one girl, Meg. I would call her every night and slip notes to her at school.

As did all of my friends, she had a steady boyfriend, Taylor. At some level, I was very jealous of him, but I acted happy for her. Once in her bedroom, I saw Meg in her slip. It hit me that as soon as she finished high school she was actually going to marry Taylor. He would know her intimately and in ways that I never could. Once sitting in a swing with her, I asked which was worse being homosexual or being a prostitute. I do not recall what she answered but obviously, I was very curious about the gay world, but had no interest in prostitution.

I read everything that I could find on homosexuality. There was not much available except passages in the Bible, which were no great help. From there I learned I was doomed to hell. I did read The Well of Loneliness with its sad ending and one or two of the Ann Bannon lesbian novels. I was intrigued by the stories of Christine Jorgenson and Jan Morrison who had undergone sex change surgery.

I knew that I was different somehow, but at that time was not at all clear about my sexual preferences. I was late maturing in that I did not menstruate until I was sixteen. Other girls would talk with each other about their menstrual periods and I was left out, again the outsider.

No one had actually described the menstrual process to me. Our health education in school was limited to non-existent. Mama, at some point, declared that when I menstruated I was not to go swimming or take a bath. I did not know what dire circumstances would occur, but until I was sixteen, it was not to be a problem.

Sixteen was also the age one could get a driver's license. From as early as I can remember I was fascinated by cars and always wanted to drive. When I was about twelve, Uncle Jennings had let me sit in his lap and steer his pickup truck on the dirt roads of Dalkeith.

Mama had bought a car, parking on the street in front of the house. I would beg her to let me start it up and move it or drive it for a short distance, such as half a block.

I learned to drive and the day I was sixteen I was an early arrival to secure a license. In my haste to begin the exam, I forgot to start the car. The examiner reminded me to turn the key. I went through the various exercises in driving and parking and passed the exam. My joy knew no bounds.

Outside of school, I found some women's basketball and softball teams and played on those. They gave me a great sense of fun and belonging. I thoroughly enjoyed the women and girls that I was playing with. I loved the uniforms and the competition. We were young and I suspect that some of my acquaintances were budding lesbians, although it was never discussed.

One of my good friends was Evelyn Creamer. She and I played on a pick-up softball team together. Once, when we were traveling for an out of town game, we stopped and picked up a new player, Joy, a pitcher. I had seen Joy once before on the opposing team of one of our games, but I did not really know her. We traveled six in the car, sixty miles to our game. Joy pitched and, as usual, I was the catcher. She had such a hard, fast pitch that I put a handkerchief in my glove to soften the catch.

I do not remember whether we won or not, but I do recall that somehow I maneuvered my way into sitting beside her on the way home. The radio was on. The announcer was giving the results of the Alabama State tennis tournament that had been played earlier in the day. I had won the doubles championship with Ruby Mays, a girl from Mississippi. The announcer mentioned my name to the great surprise of the folks in the car, since I had not told them the results. Joy said we really needed to celebrate and I invited her home with me.

We stopped by the motel where Joy's mother was the manager and she picked up some clothes. I don't know where Mama was that night except I know she was out of town. She may have been in Pennsylvania with Bud, who was playing in the Little League World Series.

First, Joy and I put on some records and danced. This was the first time I had ever danced with a girl and maybe the first time I had ever danced at all. I liked it. The night became a print-this-phenomenon. I was suspended in space not knowing what was going to happen but tingling with anticipation and excitement.

I took a bath while she waited in the bedroom. She took a bath and then joined me. We lay together on the bed as if getting ready for sleep. It was almost dawn and getting light. She leaned over and kissed me.

All of a sudden, my world shifted. I was in a life changing moment. The rusty locks on my heart clicked open. I felt a new freedom, beyond the old hurts and pain of being different. I knew I had crossed a bright line to a new sense of being. I was 17; Joy was two years older. Slim, blond, and beautiful, she was already involved with a slightly older woman.

On the Sunday after the kiss, I met her at a local swimming pool. I saw her dive off the high dive, something I had never attempted. I was enormously impressed and already head over heels in love. We only saw each other a few times after that. She continued her relationship with the other woman and I retreated into daydreams and my same old sports.

I did talk to Creamer about what had happened. She was very comforting and advised me not to worry about my feelings for Joy. I would have worried less if I had known that Creamer was also involved with a woman, something she failed to tell me at the time.

Some 40 plus years later, I had occasion to meet Joy once again. I was in Birmingham, visiting from Massachusetts, and touched base with some of the old softball crew. The woman who had been second baseman gave a party at her home and invited the teammates that were still around. Joy was there. She had been married to a man, but returned to the gay life and seemed happily involved with her long-term partner.

We reminisced and I told her how our relationship, short though it was, had changed everything for me. She remarked that bringing me out was the worst thing she had ever done in her life. I was stunned.

How could we have spent more than forty years feeling so differently about the same event?

For me, it was one of the most thrilling and precious things that had ever happened. For her, it was the beginning of a time of guilt and self-loathing about the act.

Having kissed me, a youngster (although 17), she believed she had lured me into a lesbian life. At that time, homosexuality was thought to be a crime, a perversion, a sin, a dark world to be avoided at all costs.

I tried to reassure Joy and tell her of the joy she brought me. As she was caught in the shame of homosexuality, I don't think she believed me.

During that weekend, I marched in a Gay Pride parade in Birmingham. My old friends refused to join me, afraid that they might be found out. I had marched in other parades and was from out of town; I knew I would be all right. I also knew what it meant to live in the closet and I sadly understood why my old friends could not live openly as lesbians.

Chapter 11

A High School Diary

In trying to remember my growing up days, I was reminded of some old letters that I had saved. I opened a trunk in my basement (a hoarder's paradise) that I have had since graduate school days. As I began to rummage through it, I was immediately drawn to materials that my mother prepared at my birth. There was a baby book with dates of my walking, talking, and a lock of my hair. Numerous photographs through my early years were there, too. Moreover, there was a collection of old school notebooks along with a number of letters. I began to read an old high school notebook.

During my sophomore year of high school, in 1952, (I was 15 or 16), an English teacher had us keep a notebook during the semester with entries on "What Makes Me Tick?"

I start out with, "Why am I like I am?" and go on to write that my forebears were musicians and that, perhaps, I had inherited their interests. I wrote about playing the piano and viola, noting that I have a terrible voice, and was never able to stay on key. I suspect I was thinking back on my ancestors, especially Sidney Lanier, a famous poet, who was, I am told, a great-great uncle. I wanted to write poetry like him and even tried when I was very young.

In this first excerpt, I did add in my love of sports. I wrote:

"My Monday nights are spent playing basketball and my summers playing tennis. I used to play softball but Joe Harmarth, who gave me tennis lessons last summer asked me to quit playing. Last summer I traveled around a bit to

*play tennis and this summer the MacGregor Sporting
Goods Company, which sends me new racquets, has arranged for me to play up North if I want to."*

I failed to mention that I was nationally ranked. In my next
entry I wrote:

> *"My favorite subjects in school are English and speech.
> I don't really like math at all though I've never found it dif-
> ficult. I like science, especially electronics and radio, and
> I spend my session room periods helping Mr. Youngblood
> in the science office. At auditorium, I run the slides for
> songs and live in fear of making a mistake."*

I went on to talk about my not liking people, not liking to be
in a crowd and not having many friends, nor wanting to have
them. This feels very alien to me now. I have been puzzling about
the meanings of these words in regard to what kind of kid I was.

> *"I want to be always doing something, be busy and ac-
> complishing something. I hate to be disturbed when I'm
> doing something and I like to sleep by myself. I like to
> spend my time the way I want to, doing just what I want to,
> and nothing more. I hate for a room to be disorderly and
> messy and have things out of place."*

Evidently, I was developing the obsessive-compulsive behaviors
that are with me to this day. I still like an orderly home and plan
carefully to avoid surprises. I live under an unrelenting pressure to
get things done immediately. I live with anticipatory anxiety and try
to plan well ahead to avoid upset. I am rule-bound and afraid to try
new things, never wanting to move "beyond the lines."

Unfortunately, I am either in the past or in the future, rather than living in the present with its possibilities of spontaneity and creativity. I think that as a child and as an emerging adult that I was building a shell around myself for some sort of protection. In addition, I was a bit paranoid about depending on other people either for friendship or for emotional support.

Given my chaotic experiences with my mother and the men who molested me, I believed that there were few people, whom I could trust. I wanted to be independent and involved in my own activities. At that time, I did not welcome others into my life. They might have disrupted my organized being. I wrote:

"There is one brother, smaller than I am, a cousin, also a boy age thirteen and my mother in my family. My mother works as a cocktail waitress and I do the housework. I learned to cook a few years ago and since then have cooked for the family. My day goes something like this. Up in the morning about a quarter of seven, my clothes are laid out and it doesn't take long to dress. Catch the bus at 7:25 and then ride to school. I walk the four blocks from the bus to school and go to my locker. . . . I go to Mr. Youngblood's office (and then to classes). After school, I walk back to the bus stop and then home. I get home about three forty five, clean up the house, cook supper, and do dishes, do any lessons I have, polish my shoes, set the clock, read the Bible and finally go to bed. The next day I go through the whole thing all over again."

Looking back, I see I developed a rather compulsive schedule for myself, seldom if ever deviating from it. I did not include others in my life and was essentially socially deprived. Further, I was resentful of the monotonous and unpleasant life that I led, which included little more than school and housekeeping. This likely also set me in the ways that I hate cooking and housework now.

School and sports were my salvation, although I was really hard on myself. No one proposed goals for me, but I invented them – lofty goals that I doubted then I could ever reach. I wrote:

> *"Today is Monday, the first day of a new school week and a new grading period. A time to look back over the first six weeks of school and see the mistakes I've made, the things I should have done and didn't, the things I shouldn't have done and did. A time to decide just what I can do to correct my mistakes and try to do it. A time to look ahead and try to do better. A time to read wholesome literature, hear good music, make new friends of more people and to talk less and listen more.*
>
> *I'm glad today's today. I'm glad it's not yesterday, for yesterday is always gone along with the things we'd like to forget. I'm glad today's not tomorrow for tomorrow never comes with its things I intend to do. But I'm glad today's today."*

Pretty pretentious for an intellectual 15-year-old nerd.

About mid-way through these essays, on Friday, March 14, I wrote about my family and elementary school history. I skipped over a couple of grades and then:

> *"I finished school at Avondale in 1950. As I look back now, I remember so many things that happened that seemed so important then and so trivial now. Such as the time mother made me quit playing football with the boys, the time I got a black eye playing basketball, and I always*

laugh when I remember the night I tripped over home plate playing softball and nearly broke my nose. The time I won the Poetry Festival for the southern district and how excited I was . . . my first date, my senior tea, my first piano recital, my first day of high school. I lived through them although I didn't think I'd ever make it and not there just a part of the life I've already lived, of the time that's already past and can be brought back only in memory."

Three days later on a Monday, I wrote:

"Today I don't feel good, my head hurts and I'm sleepy. Last night I tossed, turned, and didn't fall asleep until about eleven o'clock. Sometimes I wonder if life's really worth living. Why not just give up. I have always wanted to go to college and really do something worthwhile and not just 'die and be forgotten like the rest.' But, I'll never be able to work myself through eight years of college [at that time I wanted to be a doctor]. Why should I go ahead and take geometry, Latin, and French? I'll probably have to quit high school and get a job anyway before I graduate."

A month later:

"I feel good today. I don't know why but everything seems all right for the first time in a long while. The days are getting longer, the grass is getting greener and the air is getting warmer. It's perfect weather for playing tennis and, at last, it's softball season again."

In my notebook, I continued to write about summer plans, mostly thinking about playing tennis. Then I write about my job working in the library. My afterschool hours were 3:30 to 5:30, and 10 to 1 on Saturdays. I worked through the summer with longer hours. Surrounded by books, this helped to launch my life-long love affair with reading and collecting rare books.

The same entry on May 1 continued:

> *"The other night the strangest thing happened to me. I don't know just what it was or how to explain it. I was lying across my mother's bed reading 'Dawn's Early Light' and was at what I thought was a dull part. It was a part about a battle in South Carolina and I didn't like that particular part at all; so I was reading just to finish that section. My eyes were tired so I stopped a minute. As I lay there, I thought of how I was waiting. It was about 8:30 on a Friday night and I was just waiting. Waiting to go to bed; waiting for Saturday morning, waiting to get out of school for the semester; waiting to finish college. I thought, what am I waiting for and then I got scared. I don't know what I was scared of but I don't believe that I have ever been so scared before. I could feel the blood draining from my face and my hands were shaking. There was sort of a queasy feeling in the pit of my stomach and I wanted to cry. I was like that a couple of minutes and then I got all right. I didn't start reading the book again though."*

I still remember that event vividly. I still do not know its meaning. I think though that it was to warn me that I could not live just waiting for something – a message I wish I could heed. It seems like I am always waiting and not fully living in the moment. I am caught up either in the past berating myself for mistakes or bad decisions, or dwelling in the future, catastrophizing about all the things that can go wrong.

I battle with my moods, hoping for energy in down days and seeking rest in others. These varied moods have been with me through most of my life. I feel mentally and emotional stable now, but I have had serious bouts of depression and at least one bout of mania where I went out and bought three houses.

I had some real estate in North Carolina. When I sold a house there, I looked around for where to invest the gains I had made. I bought two more houses and a condominium and worked with a contractor to refurbish them. I took out big mortgages and was rapidly getting over my head in debt. Friends were concerned and my financial advisor said he would no longer work with me if I continued my extravagant spending. I was able to sell the properties without too much loss and my manic behavior diminished.

I wonder what paths my life might have taken without the history of mood swings. There have been times when I was so depressed that nothing was of interest to me. My depression was marked by a chronic sadness and an inability to feel anything.

I was filled with a psychic pain. Nothing gave me pleasure. I was able to get through the day, but it was that monotonous, steady drip, drip of inactivity when I simply wanted to shut myself away from the world.

The bouts of hypomania were accompanied by irritability. Like the adolescent who wrote that she did not want to be distracted in her everyday life, I would set myself on a steady path and become enraged if anything interfered. I was living with the pressure to hurry up and get things done. At times, my energy was boundless. I wished that I could come to some reasonable balance of moods.

So, what makes me tick? I still do not know, but I may have some clues from those early writings. I have a favorite quote from a poem by Alexander Pope. "To will implies delay; therefore now do."

I still would like to know when to seize the moment and take action. How does one live as an authentic being in the here and now? The struggle for answers has always been with me and continues to this day.

TENNIS

Top: Bonnie, a standout on the high school boys' tennis team. Above: Bonnie demonstrates a powerful serve. Right: Bonnie is ready to return service.

JUNIOR CHAMPS—Bonnie Strickland, left, and Barbara Ogle, right, teamed to capture the Junior Girls' doubles crown in the Public Parks Tennis Tournament. They beat Betty Lambert and Ellen Lively, 12-10. Miss Strickland also won the singles title, beating Miss Lively, 6-1.

BIRMINGHAM POST-HERALD
WEDNESDAY, AUGUST 2, 1950

A break in the weather finally moved the Public Parks tennis tournament back in action yesterday, but most men's matches were still behind schedule.

Graham Shanks won the junior boys singles title by blanking Al Harmon, 6-0, 6-0, and Bonnie Strickland stopped Ellen Lively, 6-1, in finals of the junior girls' division. Holmes and Bartholomew won the junior boys' doubles crown, defeating Nabors and Kirk, 6-0, 6-1, and Strickland and Barbara Ogle won the girls' doubles by beating Betty Lambert and Lively, 12-10.

Jim Adkins beat Sherry Morgan, 6-2, 6-0, for the Western senior boys' title, but has to wait on two rounds of Eastern singles.

The men's doubles are in the semi-finals, but both rounds will have to be played by tomorrow afternoon in order for the championship to be played Saturday.

The lower bracket of the Western men's singles also is behind, and the winner will have to play two rounds before tomorrow and then play Ward Wagner, champion of the upper half, before Saturday.

Scores turned in yesterday moved Jimmy Kyle out to the finals in Eastern men's singles by beating Calvin Karth, 8-7, 6-0, and Kyle and McRee went into the Western doubles finals by stopping Joe Osment Jr. and Marvin Buchanan, 6-4, 6-3. Karth and Richard Terry moved out another round in Eastern doubles by cropping Pitts and Stacks, 6-2, 6-2, and Jimmy Odum eliminated Dan Prowch in Eastern senior boys' singles, 6-3, 6-0.

Top: A 1950 Birmingham newspaper article about Bonnie and double's partner, Barbara Ogle, winning the Junior Girls' Championship title. Bonnie also won the singles crown in the Junior Girls' Championship tournament. Below: Bonnie waits her turn on the tennis court.

Chapter 12
Mama and Me

During my high school days, as I was trying to achieve some independence, my relationship with Mama became increasingly strained. She must have known of my increasing interest in women and was especially perturbed about my having anything to do with the lesbian softball team I had discovered. I had to ask her permission to do anything and she kept me to strict curfews. I was afraid to disobey.

Once I was invited by the softball team to travel with them to Atlanta for a game. I called Mama who was at work to ask her if I could go. I could not reach her but left a message. When I returned late that night, she was waiting up for me. I was grounded and could not go out or use the phone for weeks.

She was quite different when she knew that I was going to be with a boy. She was curious about my every date and would sneak around to spy on me whenever I brought a boy home.

At this time, Mama had leased a small convenience store that had a food counter. It was down the street from our house and across from the park. The store was open every day from early in the morning until late at night. I worked there, often attending the store alone. I cooked hamburgers and hot dogs with the odious task of having to clean up the greasy plates and utensils in a sweltering kitchen.

Once a sales representative came by when I was alone in the store and brought in some very small saltshakers that one could use on an outing in the park. He asked if I would like some for the store. I thought they were a good idea but I was afraid to make a decision on my own. I finally decided to purchase them for the store and waited apprehensively for Mama to return. Luckily, for me, she approved.

I did not realize it then, but she seemed to always want me under her control. I knew instinctively that I was not to make an independent decision or assert myself in any way. My last whipping occurred after I had left the store to go across the street to the park. Evidently, I stayed too long. Mama was awaiting my return with a piece of wooden molding. She whipped me through my jeans. I did not cry or let her know how much I hurt.

I did look at her in disbelief. I think perhaps she realized then that would be the last time I would let her punish me. I left the store and walked up the street toward our house. I had no other place to go. I felt helpless and confused, wondering if I would ever escape Mama and life as I knew it then.

I was only 17 and dependent on Mama. I was, perhaps, the most miserable that I had ever been. I had no answers as to how I could survive. Finally, I reverted to my old independent stance.

I was tough. I told myself I could live with this, at least for a couple of more years. I would prevail. Still, I wonder why I did not leave home sooner.

As it was, I did not really talk to other folks about the conflict and there was no one to take me in, no place to go. I also believed Mama's threat about reform school. She told me that she could announce me incorrigible and the authorities would incarcerate me. There were times I thought reform school would be preferable to living with her.

When I was younger, I had tried desperately and constantly to get Mama to let me live with Daddy. When I was about thirteen, she agreed to let me move across town to be with him. He had remarried a few years earlier and I loved his new wife, Roxie.

I joyfully made plans for the move thinking about the school I would attend and the escape from Mama. At the last minute, the plan fell through and I was not allowed to move. I was heartbroken. No reason was given, although later I suspected that Roxie did not want me exposed to my father's drinking and womanizing. I resigned myself to remaining in Mama's house, a sullen and angry adolescent. When I continued to beg to leave, Mama would again suggest the girls' reformatory. Barring that, she insisted that I stay with her until I finished high school.

On graduating high school, I was finally independent. I moved in with Creamer and her mother (Creamer's father had passed away) and paid $30 a month for a room and breakfast. Although I would visit, I would never live in my mother's house again.

I came to know Creamer much better, talking and visiting with her often. One night I ventured into her room where she was having a sleep over with her girlfriend, Dit. I sat on the edge of the bed and talked with them and was enormously surprised (and happy) when Creamer announced that she and Dit were lovers. I sure wished she had told me earlier.

I found a summer job at a local public swimming pool where I was responsible for cleaning the women's locker room, a rather odious task of mopping dirty floors and picking up used Kotex. I had always wanted a nickname and this seemed like a good time to announce that I was Bobbie. The manager figured out my ploy, however, when I once failed to respond to this new name. I reverted to Bonnie.

My pay was $100 a month. After taxes, I took home around $90. I tried to save as much as I could for college. Although hungry at times, I would skip meals that I had to pay for and refrained from buying anything but essentials. The swimming pool was located in a park in a poor neighborhood. The locals were particularly skilled in certain less than legal activities, which they taught me. I learned how to rob the vending machines in the lobby of popcorn and candy bars.

A new friend, Pete, who was on probation for statutory rape, would bring me tomato sandwiches that his grandmother made for him. When the sandwiches were not available, I would go to a corner store at the edge of the park and buy a hamburger and RC cola for 26 cents.

I took the bus to the pool in the morning but had no way home in the evening when the buses were no longer running. I was dating a boy, Bill, who had a car. He would usually take me home. We would stop and buy a barbeque sandwich. These were my meals for most of the summer.

My friend, Pete, and I became close although we were never romantically involved. Toward the end of the summer, he went to jail but we continued to stay in touch. Sometime later, I visited him in the penitentiary. He talked to me about his life there and I talked about being in college. He introduced me to some of his friends and pointed out the man who had killed the attorney general of Alabama. I was enthralled contrasting my life with his, so glad to have escaped an unhappy home life to enjoy independence and freedom.

After he was released from prison, Pete came to visit me at my college. We walked among the brick buildings and Pete remarked that they seemed similar to the buildings at the prison although without the walls. For the last couple of years, we had traveled separate paths, but we still nourished a friendship and stayed connected.

Chapter 13
College and Independence

After years of doubt and trepidation about being able to go to college, that magic time finally arrived. In the fall of 1954, I packed carefully and, alone once again, made my way to Alabama College for Women. I knew absolutely no one there. Located in the town of Montevallo in the center of the state, Alabama College was established in 1896.

Originally, the school opened not as a college, but as an elementary and high school named Alabama Girls' Industrial School. Its primary purpose was to give industrial and technical training to the girls of the state so that they might earn their own living. In the 1880s, such institutions were being advocated in the Deep South and eventually eight such schools, supported by their states, were established. Later they would become state colleges for women.

At that time, generally speaking, there were few occupations open to women. The school proposed to offer programs among others for teachers, artists, musicians, stenographers, bookkeepers, dressmakers and milliners. Total expenses for the year were $80, which covered room and board, health care, laundry and textbooks. It costs $15 to apply and between 125 and 150 girls showed up for the opening. The school was underway. Nine faculty were present with each being paid $60 a month. Within a couple of decades, there were considerably more faculty and a full four-year college curriculum had been added. The first Bachelor's degree was awarded in 1922 and the school was then officially a college.

When I entered Alabama College in 1954, the school had less than 500 students, and they were all white. The largest number had been enrolled in 1940-41 and the school had been losing students since, as had all of the women's colleges in the South.

I loved the small classes, but the lack of enrollment was to lead to a choice between bankruptcy and admitting men. I almost preferred bankruptcy but halfway through my college career, men were indeed added to the student body and the school survived. Now it enrolls about three thousand students and is one of the finest liberal arts colleges in the South.

The campus was (and is) beautiful, located on hundreds of acres with a lake and a golf course. The stately buildings are of brick and connected by brick walkways. There is an impressive auditorium, a library, and a large dining hall. My job was to wait tables in the dining hall. I began work early in the morning, served breakfast, came back again at lunch and dinner, cleaned silver on Saturday mornings and made 65 cents a day. The job, combined with a scholarship, enabled me to pay the full costs of attending college.

Because I was working, I had to come to school early to become oriented to the dining service. On one of the first days, we had a retreat at a camp house on the lake that was a part of the college. As we settled onto our cots, one of the older students kissed me good night on the forehead. There was that touching again. I liked it.

The kiss was gentle with no hint of sexuality. Not being used to being touched, I was suddenly struck with the notion that physical touching, such as this kiss, could be a special interplay of individuals coming together for a meaningful connection beyond sex and seduction.

Everything about being at Alabama College became a delight for me. I shared a room with another freshman; I had three good meals a day. My laundry was done for me and, if needed, I had good health care. Mostly, though, I gloried in the company of my female classmates and delighted in the women faculty that engaged me in the world of learning.

I immediately chose my major, Physical Education. Having given up the notion of professional sports, it never occurred to me that I would choose any other major or become anyone other than a phys ed teacher. I was delighted that I could combine my love of sports and teaching.

Most of my courses were physical education classes although I had to take freshmen English and History. I particularly enjoyed my English class and was complimented for my writing. In fact, after I wrote a paper about life in Dalkeith, my English teacher, having corrected our papers, came rushing in saying, "Class, we have a Mark Twain among us."

Physical education majors were required to take several biology courses. Our biology faculty was a young man, Gideon Nelson, and one of his classes was Field Biology. We would get up before dawn, go out into the fields, and listen for birds. We collected insects and mounted them on cardboard mats.

Dr. Nelson was also collecting water samples from the campus lake and would occasionally let me accompany him. We would float in a canoe to retrieve the samples and I asked what they were for. He said that he shared them with other biologists who were also collecting samples from other lakes to compare results. This was my first exposure to any kind of scientific investigation.

Dr. Nelson secured a cadaver, an elderly Black man, for our anatomy course. One day in class, Dr. Nelson scraped a scalpel across the cadaver's skin and said, "Look, the color isn't even skin deep."

Perhaps this was the first time I began to think seriously about race and its implications. To this point, I had never interacted personally with a Black person nor any other minority person. I was intrigued by the notion that under our skin we are all similar. Dr.

Nelson was an exciting and provocative teacher. He opened my eyes to new ways of thinking and taught me much more than biology.

I was to learn that my school was known to be a liberal bastion in the heart of the Deep South. Our female psychology professor, Katherine Vickery, went to the University of Alabama to be of assistance to the dean of women when the first Black students were to be admitted. These were the days when George Wallace stood in the schoolhouse door.

The other psychology faculty member, Herbert Eber, was involved in early integration efforts in the city of Birmingham, thirty miles up the road.

The Ku Klux Klan was active and marched around our campus. This was after one of the students at the Methodist Wednesday evening worship asked that the community pray for "brotherhood," a term the Klan took for integration.

For whatever reasons, I was drawn to the efforts of Black individuals seeking admission to a white institution to secure a college degree. Perhaps I was attuned to their struggle because of my own early dreams of attending college along with the feeling that I was an outsider, always on the margins. I also was so proud of the faculty that were doing all they could to help the Black students. Likely, these times were a precursor to my later involvement in civil rights activities.

Immediately on beginning college, I involved myself in various extra-curricular activities. The school had a radio station and I became a disc jockey. I was also interested in drama and theater, especially when I was selected to act, usually in a male role. I invariably fell in love with my leading lady and particularly enjoyed the fake kisses we exchanged.

I found myself immediately in synch with the activities of the college. I was popular and was elected a Class Favorite my freshman year. I loved my classes and was good at the sports the physical education classes entailed. These were all new experiences for me, so different from my high school days. I was happy and energized and folks seemed to respond to me differently than in my past, or so I thought. I do not know what it was about the synergy of me and my college, but I knew that I was respected and cared for. I felt a renewed sense of place and being at home in a family of friends and faculty.

Most of that excitement and pleasure at being in college had to do with being immersed in a community of women. There were few male faculty members and, aside from the dean of women, the administration was male. Beyond that, Alabama College was a bastion of women.

Women faculty ran the school and they did it very well. Being surrounded by females I felt at home, another sense of being in the right place. I also had the chance to see adult women who were successful faculty engaged in professional activities. They had been educated in the finest universities, yet they were only able to find positions at small colleges and women's colleges. We students at Alabama College were the beneficiaries. The women faculty became my role models and, for the first time, I was taken with the thought that I might be able to teach in a college setting.

The college had a homecoming tradition of having the members of the student body choose to be on either the Gold or Purple (the school colors) side. Every year, the Golds and the Purples each wrote an original play, usually with music, and competed as to who had the best production.

The crews on each side built the sets for the plays, designed the lighting, and were the actors in the plays. A Cabinet supervised the crews.

Unusual for a freshman, I was selected to be on the Gold Cabinet in charge of lighting. I was a loyal Gold throughout my college days. In my senior year, I was elected Gold Leader, one of the highest offices one could hold in the school. I just attended my sixty-second homecoming, still cheering for the Golds.

My early involvement on the Gold side gave me quick access to campus leaders. From the very beginning of my first year, I became romantically involved with some of the older students.

I suppose that like many women's colleges there were a number of romantic attachments between women. Most would experiment in college and then go on to lead a straight life. Others, like me, would find themselves to be lesbian.

Of course, this was never talked about. It was assumed that if one were found to be romantically attracted to another woman, she would be immediately expelled (and likely referred to a psychiatric hospital). Although this was not an expressed policy, it is what we students believed.

When one of our popular lesbian students disappeared from school very suddenly, we assumed it was because she had been outed to the administration. None of us ever heard from her again.

I was also enormously curious about the female faculty and gradually began to suspect that some were in lesbian relationships. Once when I was storing equipment in the gym, I heard one of the female phys ed professors call another woman faculty, "Honey." I was surprised and intrigued, adding yet another bit of information to my curiosity about the lesbian community.

My liaisons were usually short term although I considered myself deeply in love with several of the women with whom I was involved. We never talked of the future or even assumed that our relationship would continue beyond college.

I was never particularly attracted to the more masculine women. They were rather easy to identify but I was drawn to more feminine women. They were much harder to spot in terms of their romantic proclivities.

I never knew when I met someone if she would be sexually inclined toward women and attracted to me. We spent much time testing our romantic boundaries and lots of dancing around our attraction to each other.

The dance was always mysterious. I was anxious not knowing if my generally subtle advances would be accepted or rejected. I was frightened of being found out. Usually, the other and I would begin our interactions with a conversation, getting to know each other. We would advance to sharing intimacies and become close. Finally, the time would come when we would admit our feelings toward each other.

I still pretended to be straight. Although early on there were few boys to date in our small community, I did see a deaf boy from Montevallo for a while – another outsider. I also asked a neighbor boy from home to accompany me to one of our frequent dances.

When men were admitted to the college, I made friends with several of them, engaging in outdoor activities such as hiking in the countryside around the college. We also explored the limestone caves not far from the campus and competed with each other as to who would go the deepest and the farthest.

The most poignant time of my attempts at the straight life occurred when I was a sophomore. In an effort to socialize us, the college would often invite men from some of the military bases to come to the campus, meet a partner, and go to a dance.

On one occasion, I signed up for an escort. Because we often had formal dances, Mama, still hoping for a chance to feminize me more, had bought me not one but two evening dresses. I put on makeup and one of the dresses preparing myself to meet my escort. I sat in the window of my room and watched the handsome young men come to the dormitory to find their date for the evening. No one came for me. After all my efforts, by some quirk, I had not been matched with anyone. I sat in the dark, hurt and humiliated, in makeup and a dress I never wanted to put on in the first place.

As is evident, I loved being in college where I was allowed to flourish and was sometimes admired for my skills. The faculty, both male and female, were my beloved parental figures. I had good friends and a chance to become intimately involved with wonderful women. I also had the opportunity to pursue my interest in becoming a teacher.

In my senior year, I was a student teacher in the local schools. I taught physical education for the first, fifth, seventh, and twelfth grades. Once it snowed in Montevallo and the fifth grade teacher let the students go outside. Most had never seen snow before. When they returned to the classroom, the teacher had them write poems about the snow and then set their poems to music. This was my first exposure to experiential teaching and learning. I never forgot the experience and still use this particular model in my own teaching.

Occasionally, especially when the college was closed, I would spend weekends and holidays at Mama's. However, I mostly arranged to spend all of my time on campus, including summers. After my first year, I found a job in the recreation department of the town of Montevallo where the college was located. I would keep that job for four summers. My primary obligation was to be a lifeguard and teach swimming at the local creek that ran through the town. Over the time I worked there, I pulled 23 struggling swimmers to safety. I particularly enjoyed teaching swimming, especially to the Boy Scouts from some of the neighboring towns and farms. The creek was the most water they had ever seen.

In order to live in the dorms during the summer, I had to take at least one class. The one I remember the best was a Shakespeare class taught by a visiting female faculty member from the Mississippi College for Women. When I was sitting on the creek bank with little to do, I would memorize words from Shakespeare and recite them in the hot summer air. I would spend time with the kids that came to the creek and sometimes, when they were not swimming, I would play games with them and teach them chess. During the school year, in addition to my job in the college dining room, I gained access to the local movie house by distributing show programs. I also had a paper route throughout the dormitories.

However, Mama seriously threatened my livelihood not long after my sophomore year began. She suddenly appeared and said that she would pay my tuition if I gave up my job in the dining room. She explained to the dean of women that she was afraid that the stress of working along with college demands would lead me to become mentally deranged, rather like my Uncle John.

I was terrified. I begged the dean to let me keep my job, but she was impressed that Mama was offering to help. Mama did pay $60 toward my tuition but I did not quit working. As I expected, she never made another payment. Luckily, I had enough savings to get by until my summer job.

Was Mama really so determined to have me fail? I really don't think so, at least not on a conscious level. Looking back, I can see how her having me quit my job might have been an attempt at support on her part. I thought back to her telling the librarian not to allow me advanced books. In her own way, Mama was likely trying to be of help and support me, even financially. I did not see it that way then, but I am trying to remember now some of the concern she had for my well-being.

I believe she was sincere in her effort to feminize me, thinking that would lead me to have a more normal and fulfilled life. Yet, no doubt, she was frustrated at my growing independence and her lack of influence on me.

I suspect that Mama's motives were more complex than can be easily explained. At some unconscious level, I think she felt competitive with me, especially around intellectual pursuits. She would never want me to surpass her. She certainly did not have to worry about me competing with her for men, but perhaps she could control other aspects of my life. She might also have been jealous of my female friends knowing I was closer to them than to her.

Was I under stress? Possibly.

Another strange event, one that I never understood, occurred. One spring when I was playing basketball in our gymnasium, for no apparent reason I began crying uncontrollably on the court. The gym teacher quickly rescued me and sent me to the college infirmary where I rested for a while and was then let go.

While I did not make the connection at the time, this occurred very shortly before we were to go on spring break; I had no place to go except Mama's house. I did not make the connection to my earlier dissociative state although the events were likely related.

During college, I enjoyed all of my physical education classes. I took every one that was offered including camp craft and fly-fishing. Generally, I did very well, except in dance class. When asked to choreograph a dance piece, my classmates asked me to play dead.

I continued to play tennis. Although we did not play competitive collegiate sports, we had strong intramural teams. I was a fierce competitor and always won the tennis tournaments.

Again, tennis was to lead me to a new mentor. I began to play with Dr. Eber, one of the psychology professors. I beat Dr. Eber regularly at tennis and again 22 years later when we played at a psychology conference.

When I was at Alabama College, psychology was housed in the Department of Religion, Philosophy, and Psychology. The two faculty members were Dr. Eber, a clinical psychologist and Dr. Vickery, an experimental psychologist. I believe that there were fewer than half a dozen undergraduate psychology majors. I had begun to take some psychology classes along with my physical education courses and came to know Dr. Eber even better. I was most impressed when I learned that he was involved in the civil rights movement.

Dr. Eber consulted with a number of institutions across the state, including the Alabama School for the Deaf, the Alabama School for the Blind, the School for the Mentally Retarded, the Veterans Administration Hospital and Bryce, the State Psychiatric Hospital. He would often have his students accompany him on his rounds. Occasionally, he would let us give psychological tests to the residents. This meant we would have to practice administering the tests.

One of my good friends, Ginger Flowers, a psychology major, asked if I would take a practice intelligence test for her. I suspect she thought that for a dumb phys ed major the test would be short. I would not be able to answer the difficult questions so she could end early.

I agreed to take the test on the condition that she or Dr. Eber would let me know my score (they never did). I recall that Ginger administered the Wechsler Adult Intelligence Scale in my dorm room. I wanted so much to impress her. When she asked me to repeat a list of numbers, I would write them in my mind's eye on the wall of the room and then read them back off to her. Ginger and I were to become close friends and some years later, she moved to Atlanta where I was living. I stayed with her for a few days when one of my angry girlfriends was threatening to kill me.

I must have done well enough on the intelligence tests because Dr. Eber asked me to come and talk to him. He knew of my interest in psychology. I was reading books on age regression and practicing hypnosis in the dorms, frightened when it seemed to work. He encouraged me to take more classes in psychology, gave me a list of readings, and supervised me on some research projects. I began to accompany him on his consulting, traveling the dusty roads of Alabama.

One time, we approached the Veteran's Hospital where my Uncle John was a resident on the psychiatric ward. I asked Dr. Eber what caused schizophrenia. He responded, more than 65 years ago, with an answer that might still be relevant today. He said that he thought schizophrenia was a genetic or neurological condition that could be exacerbated with stress. I talked with him about my Uncle John and he listened sympathetically. I treasured our travels. Like being on the lake with Dr. Nelson, I had Dr. Eber to myself. We talked as if we were colleagues.

One day Dr. Eber called me into his office and we talked about my physical education major. He remarked that at some point I would become old and likely tired of my chosen profession. He said that perhaps I should investigate other majors, suggesting that I might find more satisfaction in living my life in the world of ideas.

On further reflection, I said that I might like to major in Philosophy. He told me to go and think some more. I came back, told him of my interest in English. He finally got to the point and asked if I had considered psychology. I remarked that I only knew two or three of the undergraduate majors and two psychologists, he and Dr. Vickery. I said something to the effect that I thought psychologists to be a bit strange. The psychology majors I knew were all a bit different, studying intensely and looking as if they were psychoanalyzing everyone they met.

He said that I would fit right in. He asked what I would make if I taught high school physical education. At the time, it would have been $2,800 per year. He said that if I applied to graduate school in psychology I might make almost that with a half time teaching or research assistantship. He reassured me that if I did not like graduate school I could always return home to teach physical education.

We laboriously filled out applications to four graduate programs, Ohio State, Purdue, Tennessee and Texas. Dr. Vickery came through the office and announced that of course I should apply to Harvard, so we added Harvard.

We had to put down a major area of interest and Dr. Eber said I should apply to clinical psychology. I asked why and he said it afforded me more options. I could teach, do research and see clients. Although I was not sure how to spell the word "clinical," that seemed like a good idea to me.

Harvard wrote back that while my grades were very good – they should have been, I had 90 hours of physical education – my major led me to be unacceptable.

I was admitted to all of the other schools but received no financial aid from Ohio State, my first choice. Dr. Eber had said that it was, arguably, the best clinical program in the country with prestigious faculty and a stellar reputation. George Kelly and Jules Rotter were among the best-known faculty members and each had written a significant and important book shortly before I applied.

We sat down and wrote a letter to Dr. Rotter noting that Ohio State was my first choice but I could not attend without financial aid. On a sunny morning in late spring on my way to play golf, I went by the campus post office. There was a letter from Dr. Rotter. I walked outside into the sunshine holding my future in my hand. I knew his answer would determine where I would be for the next four years.

Would I really live in Ohio among the Yankees in a cold climate? I opened the letter. Dr. Rotter had offered me a Research Assistantship with him, half time, for $2,400. I immediately rushed to see Dr. Eber, declined acceptance at the other schools, and eagerly responded "yes" to Dr. Rotter.

My senior year was a busy one. In addition to my classes, I was a student teacher in the Montevallo school system. Besides finishing my major requirements, I also conducted two pieces of research. One was a study of the effects of sleep deprivation. I kept several of my friends up for many hours to determine if lack of sleep would affect some cognitive tasks. Mostly, they just became cranky.

I also studied the relationship between flexibility and strength, thinking there would be little relationship. I had no mathematics or statistics in college, but Dr. Eber had me complete a factor analysis of the flexibility/strength study. This was no mean task since I had to complete it by hand. I would never actually learn much statistics, but I am an expert on factor analysis.

My physical education faculty was not altogether pleased about my choice to go to graduate school in psychology. They consoled themselves by telling me that, at least, Ohio State had a fine physical education program. Perhaps I could take some courses in that department. I never did. I was also aware of Ohio State as a football powerhouse and thought about the games I would attend. I wondered a lot about what life would be like among the Yankees. I was not frightened about the impending academic requirements, although I should have been, but I was concerned about living in a foreign culture with cold winters.

During my last summer in Montevallo, I joined a small community celebration where I presented merit badges to a troop of Boy Scouts I had taught to swim in the creek. The boys, from the poorest section of central Alabama, lived among the mines that had long since played out. Their mothers prepared lunch for us and the boys played an archrival baseball team from a neighboring town – Marvel versus Pea Ridge. I umpired the game wondering if I would ever again be in the hills of central Alabama. The field was red clay and the sun hot on my sleeveless arms. This would be my life if I stayed in the South. School teaching was familiar to me and the children appealing. Why would I leave and go to the despised North where I knew not one soul? I questioned my choices, fearful about embarking on yet another unknown venture farther from home than I had ever been before.

I had been accepted into one of the finest psychology programs in the world, an experiment for me that I did not want to forego.

The boys had pooled their money and gave me a sweater as a going away gift, a present I treasured for years. I would wear it often in Ohio thinking warmly of those precious summer days when I was, at least for a little while, a physical education teacher. I thanked the mothers and hugged the boys goodbye not knowing if I would ever walk those red clay fields again. As it turned out, I never did.

College was the greatest gift and awakening for me. I was engaged in activities I loved and surrounded by people to whom I could become close.

Those early feelings of the warmth of being touched reemerged. I began to feel comfortable in what were finally trusting relationships. I was able to share my feelings, carefully listening to others, trying to understand their world, and thereby mine.

Gradually, I was able to intimately and comfortably connect with others and I discovered my lesbian life. Alabama College was life changing for me and I will always appreciate my good fortune in being able to attend. I am also deeply honored on receiving the Distinguished Alumna Award in 1985.

On leaving college, I was consumed with thoughts of all the friends and lovers I would be leaving. It had always been assumed that the romantic liaisons we were in would never last past college days. Although I was going to graduate school, most of my friends, and the women with whom I had been romantically involved, were planning marriage.

Dr. Eber had convinced two of my friends to attend graduate school in psychology, but they were staying close to home and going to the University of Tennessee. One was my friend, Ginger, who had administered the intelligence test to me. I am eternally grateful that she chose me as her test subject.

Chapter 14
Graduate School

In August of 1958, I gathered my few belongings and prepared for the long trip north.

I furled my small Confederate flag and carefully placed it inside my suitcase so it would not get broken. I packed a book of poetry, Clods of Southern Earth, by Don West. It is now in the front of one of my bookcases so that I see it regularly. I knew I would want remembrances of home and the South. Like other poor Southerners, Black and white, I climbed up onto a Greyhound bus and joined the great migration north.

I had never had any desire to travel beyond the South. When I learned that I had been accepted into graduate school at Ohio State, I thought of Columbus and Ohio as a foreign country. I assumed that I could learn the language and become accustomed to the food, but expected that I would keep to myself until I returned home. And, I worried about snow and cold weather.

The city of Columbus was large and, to me, uninviting. Ohio State had about 25,000 students then, one of the largest universities in the country. As on other occasions of moving to new places, I knew absolutely no one. I did find an apartment across the street from the campus and joined other first year graduate students in attending classes.

One of the first things I did in furnishing my apartment was to place my small Confederate flag on my desk. The flag is about 5 by 6 inches on a small 12-inch wooden stick with a painted gold point at the top. When I was growing up in the 40s and 50s and beyond, it was sold perhaps at every drug store, dime store and souvenir shop in the South. More than 65 years has taken its toll. The cloth is torn, the threads frayed, and the colors faded. Yet, the stars and bars are fresh in their symbolism.

On arriving in Ohio, I found myself surrounded by Yankees and Republicans. As soon as I could, I found another southerner to room with. It was of no importance to me that she was Black. More importantly, we both had double names, ate the same food, and spoke the same language. Completely oblivious to whatever feelings she might have had toward the flag, I would sit for long hours studying the psychology that was as unfamiliar to me as the land to which I was exiled.

Occasionally, I would look at the flag, an adult security blanket, recalling long, lazy evenings back home where folks sat on the front porch, talked of the day's events, and watched children play. I thought of summer time, fishing on the river, the most political and bipartisan event of interest being whether I would catch a catfish or a blue gill. The flag reminded me of a simpler life, a comfortable fantasy of gracious, well-mannered folk fiercely loyal to family and place. It never occurred to me to reminisce about my relationship, or lack thereof, to Black people. It was a long time before I realized that the flag was a symbol of white supremacy.

In one of my first year classes, the instructor mentioned Carl Rogers. I knew I had heard the name and thought he was perhaps a minister. In the front of the room, Esther Kassoy said that she had known "Carl" at Chicago. The instructor mentioned B.F. Skinner. Again, I had heard the name but knew nothing of his work. Another student mentioned that he had studied with "Fred" at Harvard. I knew I was in over my head. From that day forward, I said little or nothing in class.

I did, however, have one piece of intellectual good luck. In an assessment laboratory class, we were learning about a non-verbal intelligence test. The task was to look at three items and determine in what way they were conceptually similar. In one question, the items were a clock, a watch, and a tree that had been cut down. I immediately recognized that the rings in the fallen tree, along with the watch and clock, indicated time. I announced the answer, which no one else knew, pleased that my southern outdoor adventures had taught me something the citified Yankees had yet to learn.

The clinical program was perhaps unique in the diversity of the faculty and students that were accepted. Although all male, the faculty included an existentialist, a phenomenologist, a psychoanalyst and three social learning theorists. While women and minorities were not usually accepted into many graduate programs, the Ohio State clinical program did accept a few.

In my class, there was a Black woman (my roommate) and an Egyptian woman. Many of the students were Jewish, but the program also had a Catholic nun and, I think, a Catholic priest. This diversity came about primarily through the efforts of Jules Rotter.

George Kelly was against admitting women, whom he saw as simply occupying a man's place, assuming they would marry and drop out. Rotter would ask Kelly to tell him which women would marry and then he would not admit them.

I believe Dr. Rotter admitted me because he thought I was Black. A kid named Bonnie Ruth from a heretofore never heard of Alabama College must be Black. When I asked him about this, he would laugh and say, "I never thought you were Black, but I knew you were culturally deprived."

I made close friends with other students in my class, several of whom went on to become distinguished psychologists. Without a car, I had to depend on them for travel once a week to our various practicum placements including a fifty-mile trip to the Veteran's Administration hospital (VA) in Chillicothe, Ohio.

I recall on one of our trips we talked about whether we would ever become famous. The men could easily note psychologists that they would like to emulate but we could not think of any famous women psychologists. We finally decided that my role model could be a psychiatrist, Karen Horney. We had all heard of her.

We tried to support each other. As I mentioned, I was quiet in classes and intimidated by the other students and the faculty. Since I had taken no math or statistics in college, I struggled through the required graduate stat courses. We also had to be proficient in a foreign language, so I reverted to my high school French.

I certainly never distinguished myself by brilliant answers in the classroom, but I did do well in a series of required seminars on various aspect of psychology beyond clinical. Only one person passed all of the seminars, which numbered about a dozen, but I was the next who had only failed one – a class on learning.

After this performance, the faculty seemed to take me more seriously. I think they were also impressed with my early involvement in research. My first research presentation during my second year was at the Ohio State Psychological Association convention. Along with faculty, I was to publish several papers in well-respected journals before I graduated. This was particularly gratifying to me since the publications were a mark of success in graduate school and precursors to an eventual job.

My master's thesis advisor, Doug Crown, was a young assistant professor who had only recently joined the faculty. He was developing what would become the Crown-Marlowe Social Desirability Scale, an assessment instrument to measure need for approval.

My thesis was an investigation of whether the need for approval scale was related to conformity. We did find a correlation and I presented my results at a professional conference. The study was published with Crown in a prestigious journal. We also conducted another published study in which the Social Desirability

Scale predicted the premature termination of psychotherapy. Much of my research, however, involved Rotter's Internal versus External Control of Reinforcement Scale (IE). This instrument was designed to elicit the degree to which the respondent expects that the events that happen to him or her are a result of his or her behavior rather than luck, chance, and/or powers beyond one's control.

My dissertation, under Rotter's direction, was an attempt to predict verbal conditioning and extinction as a function of learning without awareness. I also considered the effect of internal/external control beliefs and need for approval. The results of the experiment were significant and the study eventually published.

I suspect that my predominant interest in internal versus external control was because I was working with Dr. Rotter who developed the concept. Yet, I have no doubt that my interest was also piqued by my own concerns about control.

How fascinating that one's behavior could be predicted by their beliefs. I was continually thinking about how thoughts influenced behavior. I have continued to reflect on my needs for control, never really coming up with a satisfactory answer to a balance of control and lack thereof.

In regard to my need for approval research, I recognized that I had worried most of my life about being judged and found wanting. Maybe the need for approval scale could give me some clues as to when I was being too much influenced by my need to be liked by everyone.

The IE scale was prominent in one of my most important studies. Pearl Mayo Gore, my early roommate, and Dr. Rotter gave the scale to a large number of Black male college students. The experimenters asked the participants to what degree they would sign a petition in support of civil rights, march in a demonstration, take a Freedom Ride across the South, or do nothing.

As hypothesized, the more internal the subject, in contrast to the external subject, was more likely to answer that he would be more involved in significant social actions. Gore and Rotter wrote up the study and submitted it to the most prestigious journal in the field. The editor rejected it saying there were no behavioral components, simply paper and pencil answers.

Later I would repeat the study with actual members of the Southern Nonviolent Coordinating Committee (SNCC) and a control group of Black college students. SNCC members were heavily involved in civil rights activities throughout the South. Many had been arrested. As hypothesized, the SNCC members were significantly more internal than the control group. I wrote up the study and sent it to the same journal. The editor rejected it saying that Gore and Rotter had already conducted the study. Mine was eventually published in the Journal of Social Psychology and became a Citation Classic, a most heavily cited article in its area. As far as I know, the study was the first to predict social action from a personality variable.

Although much of my research activities through my professional career were conducted in traditional areas, those that brought me the most acclaim were outside of regular channels.

Even though I did not realize it, my interests were in answering those questions that had always been personal for me. How do disadvantaged people overcome adversity? What are the personal characteristics of women, African-Americans, and LGBTQ folks that allow them to achieve success? How does one adapt and flourish in a world marked by prejudice and discrimination? Why are women twice as likely to be depressed as men?

I never thought of myself as working beyond psychology's research constraints. Only now, I realize that my research was considered unconventional. Here was at least one area in which I was able to escape conformity and work beyond the boundaries.

In 1989, I received an Award for Distinguished Contributions to Psychology in the Public Interest. The citation reads:

"Strickland's career path is marked by the trails she has blazed, legitimizing the scholarly study of previously ignored areas important to persons whose interests were marginalized. She has been willing to conduct research in unpopular and difficult arenas. The result is that she has not only increased society's understanding of previously neglected populations but gave the message that the field when confronted with good scholarship will expand to accommodate such work. She has devoted her career to helping the discipline of psychology embrace diversity."

Chapter 15

Social Life

During my senior year of college, I had been seeing a wonderful young woman, Joan. She was engaged to be married but we still carried on an affair. She decided to attend Ohio State as a graduate student in social work and joined me at the beginning of my second year there.

She was blond, blue-eyed, and immediately attractive to my male colleagues and the fraternity men who lived next door. She was fun to be with and we reminisced about our time at Alabama College. We enjoyed the attention we received from being two Southerners in the cold North.

We were, of course, completely closeted about our relationship. She began to date men and was out the night of my birthday, a time that I had hoped she would spend with me. I went into a state in which I thought I heard voices telling me to kill her.

About this time, one of my friends came over to visit and became immediately alarmed at my condition. She asked if she should take me to an emergency room. I believed that if I were admitted to a hospital, I would shut down and never leave.

Slowly, I calmed down and began to feel normal again. This was the third of my mental "episodes" and was yet another marker of the beginning of my adult history of depression and occasional bouts of mania.

Joan began to see a dark, handsome, Latino male, very different from her blond haired, blue-eyed fiancé, Jim. She was determined that she would break up with Jim when he returned from his service in the Army. At his return, Jim responded to Joan's announcement by saying that he could use some time away, maybe stay in the North and be independent for a while. When faced with the thought of possibly losing him, Joan quickly backtracked. They returned home and were married a few months later and remained in a long, happy marriage with children.

I was one of Joan's maids of honor at the wedding – a horrendous experience of trying to align myself with the straight world while my heart was breaking. The masquerade was necessary in a world in which one could not be open and yet another painful reminder of the often heartache of being gay in a straight world.

During my second year in graduate school, I did meet a fellow student who was a lesbian. Although we were never involved romantically, we carefully danced around each other before we each admitted our attraction to women. Through her, I met another lesbian, her ex-lover, and we had a brief affair. Otherwise, I did not really know or meet other lesbians until my internship year.

Still trying to lead a "straight" life during graduate school, I dated any number of young men, usually only once or twice. I knew that I was attracted to women but I was still wondering about the straight life and if I would ever fit in.

Perhaps the right man would come along. By dating, I was also trying to disguise my homosexuality. I was aware of my attraction to women but I was still struggling to be in the straight world. My dating men was likely an experiment to see where I really belonged.

I did become enamored of one fellow student. We went out several times. I enjoyed being with him and, as the relationship developed, we became more serious. He was a lovely person, gentle, thoughtful and kind. He was not sexually aggressive; in fact, there was no sex at all.

We spent more and more time with each other, finally talking of marriage. We became engaged. I met his parents and he met Mama. The engagement was announced, with my picture, in his hometown newspaper. He gave me a star sapphire for an engagement ring, one that he had found in Burma where he had lived with his family for a while. We picked out silver and china and determined that we would set a wedding date sometime in the future.

The feelings of being engaged were almost surreal. I could not believe that I might finally join the straight world as a married woman. I was glad to be affirmed and congratulated for the engagement. I really did not think much about my leaving the lesbian life. I simply assumed that I would be happy in the marriage and, thus, not attracted to women. Mostly, I was filled with love for the normality of the engagement. I was finally a full participant in the straight world; I was caught up in the feeling of being "normal." Looking back, I think now that I was in big time denial.

Fortunately, we came to our senses. We never really argued, but once, in a restaurant we had our first spat. I don't remember the details but it had something to do with our choice of salad dressing. We talked later, admitting that we were not ready to marry, and broke off the engagement. I returned his ring and recall the relief I felt the morning after we decided to part. He never married, but became a successful psychologist and eventually adopted a young son.

Having tasted the straight life for a while, I realized that my relationships with men would never match the strong, emotional attraction I felt toward women.

I desperately searched for someone. One of my supervisors in my internship, Joyce, was a lovely woman social worker, ten years my senior. I thought her beautiful, with her dark hair and blue eyes. We gradually talked and admitted our attraction toward each other.

At that time, she was with another woman. As we became romantically involved, she broke up with her lover and we moved in together. When I graduated, Joyce and I moved south to Atlanta.

She found a position as a social worker and I settled happily into a university position. We immediately bought a house together. Like my mother, I was a young homeowner – well half a homeowner – at the age of twenty-three.

At first, Joyce and I were caught up in moving and decorating our new home. Primarily at her urging, we bought expensive furniture, silver, and china. We had a formal dining room, although we seldom had visitors. Mostly, we spent our time breeding and showing dogs.

The house sat on a couple of acres of land with a small barn, an ideal spot for a kennel. Joyce raised Irish setters and I German shepherds. We spent our weekends at dog shows all through the South. We were in Birmingham the weekend of the church bombing that killed four little Black girls. We were just passing through but were close to the site of the church.

Although we were doing nothing wrong, the police, probably because of the shepherds in the car, pulled us over but soon let us go. I remember being stunned at the police presence, the soldiers and tanks in the streets of my old hometown.

Joyce and I were together for about two and a half years. After our time spent settling into Atlanta, we began to turn our attention toward each other and found the relationship wanting.

We did not have many friends and knew almost no lesbians. As time went on, she began to be concerned about being lesbian and became consumed with Catholic guilt. She also became quite jealous of my benign relationship with Luis, a young male Mexican college student who had bought one of my dogs.

Luis and I often spent time together at dog shows showing our shepherds. Joyce had always been suspicious of my friends and she simply could not understand my friendship with Luis.

There was no third party in the breakup with Joyce. We just found ourselves quite different in interests and needs. I was more outgoing, wanting to engage in more social activities. I was tired of us spending all of our time together working around the house or in the kennel. We began to argue and she asked me to move out. It was with some relief that we separated.

I lost touch with Joyce after our breakup and only recently began to wonder what had happened to her. I googled her name and was sad to learn that after battling cancer, she had died in 2010 at age 83. From her obituary, I learned that she had moved to the North Georgia mountains for the last years of her life. She continued to be a very successful breeder of Irish Setters. Her kennel, Gavingarth Kennels, produced a champion dog, Heather, who won Best of Breed at the Westminster Dog Show. Joyce left a sister and four Irish Setters. The obituary had no mention of a companion.

Chapter 16
Clinical Adventures

In addition to our academics and research, graduate students in clinical were immediately immersed in assessment and psychotherapy with clients. In my placement at the VA hospital, I saw severely mentally ill patients. This was also the case in my practicum placement at the university psychiatric hospital. Further, I was involved in the psychology department's clinic, seeing outpatients.

The clinical program was devoted to educating and training us for academic careers, but we also received excellent clinical training. These were the early days of clinical psychology, only a decade past the first conference to establish education and training standards.

George Kelly and Julian Rotter, distinguished psychologists who were on the clinical psychology faculty at Ohio State, were participants in this conference that was held for two weeks in Boulder, Colorado in 1949. Participants in the conference determined that to receive a Ph.D., clinical psychologists, among other requirements, would be trained as both scientists and clinicians, complete a one-year pre-doctoral internship, and finish a dissertation. The graduate clinical program at Ohio State was an exemplary scientist-practitioner model, and trained a significant proportion of the emerging leaders in the field.

As a VA trainee, I completed part of my pre-doctoral internship at the VA hospital in Palo Alto, CA. This was a very prestigious appointment although I was not fond of traveling across country to yet another place where I knew no one.

I was assigned to a ward of chronic schizophrenic male veterans where I conducted both individual and group therapy. Therapy on the ward was predominantly psychoanalytic and directed by a psychiatrist and a head nurse. Other staff included my supervisor, a psychologist, Ben Finney, a social worker and several residential aides.

One day in supervision, Dr. Finney noted that I was very quiet in the group meetings that were held for all of the patients and staff. He asked if I was perhaps intimidated by the head nurse, a rather forceful figure on the ward. I answered that I simply didn't have anything to say. I had been simply sitting and observing the group.

Dr. Finney said that might indeed be the case, but he wanted to be certain that I felt free to speak up. He then asked if I had considered going into psychotherapy myself. When I blanched, he quickly said, "Now, don't get all worried and concerned. In my way of thinking, psychotherapy is like a college education. You will learn more than you could ever imagine. If given the opportunity, why shouldn't you take advantage of it?"

Since then, I have always thought that this was among the best advice one could ever receive about entering psychotherapy.

Methods of psychotherapy have changed significantly since those days. With the event of shorter duration of treatment and emphasis on the here and now of cognitive restructuring, therapists are less likely to delve into the client's history and personal development.

However, my placement in a psychoanalytic setting focused on the effects of the unconscious. I was amazed at how the group leader could lead patients past their overt behavior and investigate more deeply held motivations.

For instance, one patient reported that he was late returning to the ward after a visit outside simply because of missing a bus. The group leader encouraged him to say more about what he had been feeling. Turns out, the patient was thinking about escaping from the hospital and thought his being away from the ward was the ideal time to leave.

Without delving into his feelings, we would never have known about his ambivalence about being on the ward or his wish to elope. I have always been grateful for my, although brief, exposure to the power of the unconscious and its defense mechanisms.

After the summer in California, I returned to Columbus to complete my internship on the outpatient unit of the state psychiatric hospital. A couple of months after I returned, I received a letter from Dr. Finney. He mentioned that one of the aides on the ward had been writing a book and suggested I read it as I would recognize some of my old patients. He went on to say that he thought the book was awfully hard on Lois, the head nurse transformed into Nurse Rachet.

Lois was indeed a formidable figure. Coming from the military, she stalked through the ward like a drill sergeant attending to every detail. Her demeanor was as starched as her white nurse's uniform and cap. In spite of her authoritarian style, she was kind to the patients.

I was scared and in awe of her. I tried to keep my distance and we had few interactions. I read the book. It was none other than Ken Kesey's, One Flew over the Cuckoo's Nest. Kesey had been a residential aide on the ward and introduced the world to the woman I once was afraid of.

The experiences in Palo Alto gave me my first insights about psychotherapy's impact. In another letter, Dr. Finney wrote to tell me of the reactions of some of the patients I had seen in group therapy. One confessed to having been in love with me. Others commented on my warmth and concern for them. They said they missed me a lot. I had no idea that I had made such a difference in their lives.

My days at the Columbus internship were spent doing psychological assessment and psychotherapy with outpatients. I also saw an inpatient diagnosed as manic-depressive (now called bipolar). I became intrigued by bipolar disorder, likely trying to understand my own mood swings. I had always been interested in working with severely disturbed patients, probably in an attempt to understand my Uncle John.

The first bipolar patient I had observed was presented at case rounds. A list of symptoms was listed on a blackboard and then covered with a screen. The patient was very agitated and impulsively moving around. He noticed the blackboard and lifted the screen. He then went through each symptom noting whether it was true for him or not. At the end of the session, he was markedly distressed and treated with the latest therapy of the time, being immersed in cold water.

My supervisor for the next bipolar patient I saw was psychoanalytic in his approach. He believed mania to be a defense against depression. This particular patient was a married, middle-aged homemaker with several children. Her husband's brother, likely an alcoholic, had recently moved in with the family. He was something of a slob. The patient said that she had observed him in a drunken state urinating in the living room. One evening, having worked hard to prepare supper for the family, her brother-in-law said something disparaging about the food. The patient snapped and began to chase him around the dining room table with a butcher knife. She was subdued and brought to the hospital.

I began to see her as a patient and was encouraged by my supervisor to have her "cover her feelings." In no way was I to try to uncover any deep-seated psychological issues. We would bind her up psychologically as best we could and send her home.

I kept thinking there was more that we could do than release her back into her dysfunctional situation but we had few therapeutic tools at that time. Those were the days before drugs were readily available. We did have pharmaceutical sales representatives come to the hospital to talk about their products, but they admitted that no one knew how psychotropic drugs worked.

In my upcoming role as a clinician, I thought I could benefit by being on the other side of the desk so I considered entering therapy. My first foray into treatment, however, was a disaster.

I began to see one of my supervisors, a kind, and gentle humanist. We were only together for a few weeks, but the clash of supervision and therapy was too destructive. We now consider it unethical for supervisors to take on students in therapy. However, these were the early days of clinical psychology and ethical standards were just developing.

In addition to the clinical skills I learned at the psychiatric clinic, I was also exposed to new theoretical approaches to psychotherapy.

At Ohio State, although the clinical faculty was diverse in their theoretical models, the prevailing approach was social learning theory. George Kelly did teach us his personal construct theory and the fixed role therapy that he developed but most of our psychotherapy supervision was behavioral in nature.

My internship at the outpatient clinic exposed me to experiential therapy and Fritz Perls, the father of Gestalt Therapy. These were quite different psychotherapy models and I found myself fortunate to learn about them. I would incorporate aspects of these theories into my future clinical work although I remained rather behavioral with forays into psychodynamic approaches.

COLLEGE GRAD • PROFESSOR • LEADER

Chapter 17
A Memorable Client

Jay walked through the halls of the Clinic as if he owned the place. Tall and lanky, he was impeccably dressed, looking as if he had just stepped from the pages of a fashion magazine. His suit was well pressed, his tie knotted properly, his shoes highly polished. His hair was coiffed in the latest style, with a curl dangling mischievously on the middle of his forehead.

No one would know – and that is the way he wanted it – that his languid pace was a desperate attempt to escape his demons.

His general physician had referred Jay to our clinic. He had gone to the doctor because of headaches, intestinal distress, "nervousness," and other illnesses that the doctor could not diagnose. Finding no physical reasons for Jay's ailments, the doctor referred him for psychiatric treatment.

At the intake, Jay talked of his need to travel and some general dissatisfaction with his life. He said little about his drinking and fighting of which he had a long history. He had been traveling around the country and settled into Columbus because a traveling companion was from there. He enjoyed access to the university, slept in fraternity living rooms, and ate whenever he could. At the time he came to the clinic, he was working in a shoe store. He never held a job for long.

Jay wanted to be a poet and had already begun writing. His presentation at the clinic was that of an angry, young misfit who could not settle himself or find a life role. Jay was 23, as was I, when I began to see him in therapy.

Before the referral to me, Jay had completed an intake interview with a social worker. She shared some of his family history but it was sparse.

I knew little of Jay when I began to see him. I did learn that he never knew his father and in his early years he was raised by his mom and a stern grandmother. He was expelled from a military school after he assaulted the headmaster who, Jay said, attempted to molest him.

His mother remarried and Jay spent a year living in Europe with her and his stepfather. He joined the U.S. Army in 1955 along with 30 ex-Legionnaires to escape the French draft. He recalled that in the service, he espoused a somewhat neo-Nazi philosophy and had a bit of a following among the soldiers. After three years in the service, he was dishonorably discharged for fighting and disorderly conduct.

My supervisor remarked that Jay presented as a sociopath and doubted that he would stay in therapy. In contrast to my bipolar patient, my supervisor encouraged me to try to develop a close relationship with Jay early on, uncover his underlying feelings, and keep him in treatment as best I could.

Jay and I met for the first time on February 17, 1961 and I was immediately struck by his anger and negativism, which he tried to cover. No matter what subject we broached, he was critical and made an opposite point. He did seem motivated for treatment, always arriving promptly and quickly becoming engaged in conversation. He did, however, verbalize much resistance to being in therapy. He noted that he fought depending on another person and said therapy was conforming to a set of norms in which he did not believe.

I saw Jay twice a week. He continued his appointments and often came to his session a half hour or an hour before his slotted time. He said that he was not interested in treatment but did enjoy talking to me. He asked to see me socially and said that he felt "betrayed" that I would not date him.

We talked of his feelings of dependency on women and his belief that he cannot trust them, nor anyone for that matter. Prominent in our therapy was his perception of the world as a cruel and hostile place. He appeared to desperately crave love from others but could not bring himself to trust anyone. Nor did he let other people get to know him, as he feared they would not like him.

By the end of March, Jay was talking of how confused he was, how he was unable to hold a job, and how his therapy hours were the only things that seemed important to him. He was involved with a married woman and argued with himself as to whether he should continue to see her. He said that she gave him money, took care of his clothes, and was asking him to run away with her. He was tempted but knew he did not love her and wanted to continue in treatment. In addition, there was the question of whether she was pregnant with his child.

By the end of April, Jay became increasingly upset. At times, he went into uncontrollable rages. He was fearful that he might hurt someone or be hurt. He said that he would like to get away for a long rest. We discussed the possibility of hospitalization. I referred him to a staff psychiatrist who told Jay that he should straighten up and get a job. Concerned that he was deteriorating, I administered a battery of psychological tests. That was May 3.

As expected, Jay was very bright but his Rorschach was clear evidence of a cognitive and emotional breakdown. He saw a man being pulled apart by two female figures who were playing with his insides, a cat squashed on the highway, a rabbit torn apart. He saw dragons playing do-si-do with pink colors suggestive of cotton candy. He saw monsters injecting embryos with sickness and disease. In my session with Jay the day after testing, he was extremely upset, shaking and crouching on the floor.

On May 15, Jay called and said that he had been in his bedroom for four days. He felt as if he should go into a hospital. We immediately set up an appointment that day for a session with a psychiatrist. When he arrived to see me, Jay was agitated, confused, incoherent and with much flight of ideas. This time, after a session with a psychiatrist, the psychiatrist reported that Jay was the "craziest person" he had ever seen. Arrangements were made for hospitalization.

Jay was hospitalized for about six months. He was then released to live with relatives in a suburb of Atlanta. After he moved south, we began a correspondence. Along with asking for advice, he wrote that during our time together, he thought me unusual, even strange.

> *"All the time that you were helping me to try and see things, I was trying to analyze you. I gave up. You had a distant aura or must it be that way with your 'cases.' When I trust someone, as I did you, I have to and I did remain on my tiptoes and fingertips all the time. Always a tingling little feeling of fear lurked in my subconscious and I watched on guard and apprehensively for the first sign of betrayal or nonchalant indifference. I found none of this abomination in you. You are the one person I have ever trusted. I was awakened in absolute horror one morning to this profound realization that you are the only one in my twenty-three years. I resolved to trust someone else although this is so difficult. I try not to hate. I know that it will eventually destroy me and, God knows, even much worse than that, MAIM me, CRIPPLE me if I allow myself to be dominated by it. I'm trying not to sound as I did in your office, but, of course, I will anyway."*

Jay then went on to write that in the hospital, a resident physician (he called him an internal plumber) told him that he was an "emotional cripple." He asked what I thought and then underlined: *"I don't think that I am crippled."*

He ended the letter with,
    "How shall I close? 'All my trust?' 'Love?' Even perhaps 'All my love?' 'All my etc., etc.?' Just simply – regards or sincerely or something like that. But all that has been done to death – so I'll just say that I am looking forward to your letter with much feeling."

We wrote a few more times and then as luck would have it, within a year or two, I took a position at Emory University in Atlanta. Through the years that followed, Jay and I would occasionally meet for coffee or tea on the Emory campus. He was writing poetry and was a visiting lecturer at Emory. He continued to work odd jobs, such as telemarketing, and began to teach writing seminars. Although he never married, he was raising a son who had been abandoned to him by a girlfriend.

Through the years, with his permission, I used Jay's assessment data as a teaching tool in my classes. In the fall of 2014, I began to wonder what had happened to him. I Googled him and was amazed to learn that he was a poet of considerable renown. He had published more than 400 poems in anthologies, books, and national and international magazines such as Harper's and the New Yorker. He had received many awards and been billed as the most widely published, least recognized working poet in America. Building, perhaps, on his lack of trust in others, Jay writes about the "inherent loneliness of the human spirit." His poetry is about the misfits and the downtrodden. He writes of being an outsider watching others, isolated in the world he portrays.

Entranced, I decided to try to contact him. I had no luck with finding an email address but by chance dialed 411, gave the operator his last known residence from Emory days, asked for his phone number and received it. I decided to call. We connected and had a long conversation. Jay seemed pleased to have heard from me and brought me up to date on his life. His girlfriend, who had abandoned their infant son to Jay, returned for the child when he was six. Jay refused to let her have him and raised him as a single dad. The son is now married with three daughters, each of whom is successful in her own right. Jay sees them often.

Jay said that he had held a number of jobs and had some success in real estate. He had been hospitalized three more times and I asked how he was able to escape his psychosis. He said that he decided that the psychiatrists were all crazier than he was. He simply determined not to be crazy again. He also told me of some of his escapades as a young man.

Evidently, he and the mother of his son, Delores, had a long and tumultuous relationship. At one point, he was in jail resulting from a charge of domestic abuse. A buddy told him that one of the men who had just been released from jail was trying to find Delores, a beautiful and attractive woman. Jay said the next morning he climbed over a wall, went into town, and beat up the fellow. He then returned to the jail that evening entering the same way he had escaped. After one prison episode in South Carolina, a judge told him to leave the state and never return. Return he did with a notice in the paper that he was a poet in residence. He hopes the judge saw the article.

After our telephone conversation, we continued to correspond. I was, of course, interested to hear his reactions to the long-ago psychotherapy. Jay said that he had been "one sick puppy" and was not yet a "cured man." He remarked that he is still a bit of an emotional cripple, a stance he vehemently denied when he was twenty-three.

He talked of his anger and violence from before. He said that looking back he does not recognize that person now. He confessed that there are times when he misses "the edge" of that anger, but not the results.

He said he changed considerably when his son started walking toward him and called him Dada. He wrote, "I knew what it was like to grow up without a father and all that it cost me. I didn't want that for him."

Jay said he still employs what he calls "healthy paranoia" in his dealings with other people. Concerning me, he added that he has carried the memory of those days and our conversations throughout his life. I remarked that when I met him he was impeccably dressed. He responded that his attire was a cover up of the disheveled mess that he was.

He said he could not have been more "lost" when he walked into my office. The help and advice I gave him was the impetus for his survival of a life that, until that point, was fragmented and rejection filled.

He remarked that there are certain people you meet who you remember and take with you. Occasionally, you call upon them in memory. I was that person in his life. He told me he was grateful I was there for him at that particular junction in his life – even though flirting was to no avail. He thanked me for my emails, saying that my words meant so much to him because he felt as if I really knew him. He noted he didn't realize how much trouble he was in and how I saved him.

I had occasion to be in Atlanta, still Jay's hometown, in early 2015 and we met for lunch. We were much changed after 50 years, but still enjoyed that intimate and precious camaraderie of two people who had once been therapist and patient. During that lunch, he gave me two of his books that I treasure as much as I do a Christmas present he sent me later, a poem called Christmas Cards.

CHRISTMAS CARDS
For Bonnie Strickland

They always started coming,
one, two—three in the mailbox,
like snowflakes on an old card
from the 40s and 50s, from this

cousin, that one, my aunts and uncles.
And then as I got older, they slowed
down each year from an avalanche
to a trickle, dribbling in one at a

time, and then they stopped. They
were all gone, including most of
my old friends. But once in a while
like a sparkling gift, a glossy

snowed-in card appeared from
a name that I knew, even if it
was from my insurance agent,
my dentist, or the neighbor down

the street. It was a card full of
sparkles, and from someone still
alive, wishing me Merry Christmas
with a scene of painted snowflakes,

a reindeer drawn sleigh full of
presents, and driven by Santa Claus,
or Three Wise Men and a babe in
a manger, and in the corner of

the card, there was always a
small house banked up by drifts
of snow, with one yellow light
glowing, left on just for me.

Chapter 18

Emory: My First Faculty Position

It was assumed that graduating students in my clinical program would become academics. However, in 1962 when I received my Ph.D. and interviewed with several distinguished universities, they were not hiring women. I still have the letter I received from the clinical director at one respected university. He said that while my record was very good they had decided to hire a man (underlined) instead.

I was not surprised. This was a time when women were not welcomed into the academy. I simply knew my job search would be more difficult because I was a woman.

By mid-summer of 1962, I was still without employment. Dr. Rotter was consulting with Emory University in Atlanta, where there was a proposal to develop a graduate clinical program. They needed faculty and I needed a job. Emory made me an offer and I was able to return south where I spoke the language and appreciated the culture. Most importantly, I finally became the teacher I had long wanted to be.

Emory was an all-male school until 1953. When I arrived there, less than a decade later, there were very few women faculty. Women were in the Nursing School but there were only two or three in the college. Emory was completely segregated having no Black students or faculty.

Back then, I did not think much about the lack of women (or Blacks for that matter.) I now realize how much I could have learned if, as a young woman professor, I had female mentors. We were all living in a time when women were supposed to marry and raise a family.

As always, I felt marginalized and outside of the mainstream.

However, I was happy and successful in my job. I had many friends in the gay community as well as a number of straight men and women. At Emory, my male colleagues were supportive and kind, but I could have used advice and support from senior women faculty. No one on the faculty was out as gay. The only mention of homosexuality occurred several years later when the police arrested a gay male professor caught in a compromising situation. He was immediately fired.

My professional life at Emory involved teaching, research, and clinical work. I taught undergraduate and graduate students. I was also on the staff of the Psychological Services Center, a resource for students needing academic, vocational counseling and psychotherapy.

As expected, I loved teaching. My initial offerings were Abnormal Psychology and Personality Theory. The students were bright and motivated, with most of the men thinking about a career in medicine. Many of the women were still looking for husbands. I struggled to be a good teacher and eventually received an Outstanding Teaching Award.

I was not always comfortable in the classroom. The students were all white and almost all came from affluent backgrounds. Fraternities and sororities were strong, student dress fashionable, and student vacations spent in exotic places.

This was not a background in which I felt at ease. I did not belong. I recall in one class, I mispronounced the word Arab with an emphasis on the first A. I knew better than to say police or Detroit but I was never sure when I might make a mistake in punctuation or dress for that matter.

Some of the students were very impressive. As I mentioned before, I became close to one young man, Luis, one of the only Mexicans in the school, another outsider perhaps.

We began doing some research together and published a paper

on prejudice between Black and white individuals. Luis had bought one of my dogs to show. We went to dog training classes together and to dog shows. After Luis' graduation, we stayed in touch for decades. He became a very successful president at a large research university and I visited him there. We sat in his elegant dining room on the campus, as we reminisced about our early times together while staring out the windows at the many new buildings and facilities built on his watch.

As was expected of a young professor, I immediately became involved in considerable research. This included the study on the prediction of social action that I mentioned earlier. The other seminal study of which I am most proud was research within the gay and lesbian community in Atlanta.

I was an advisor to two male graduate students, closeted gay men, although I did not know that at the time. We began to recruit gay men and lesbians to ask about aspects of their lives. Finding gay folks was particularly difficult because no one was out. Lesbians were especially hard to find. We began with friends and finally assembled a large sample of gay men and lesbians along with heterosexual men and women. The sample was all white and mostly middle class. We found no differences in the emotional and mental health of the self-identified gay men and lesbians when matched with heterosexuals.

Results from the male sample were a replication of earlier research by Evelyn Hooker. She had found no differences between gay men and heterosexual men in their presentation of pathology on projective tests of "abnormality."

Ours was the first to demonstrate that lesbians did not differ from heterosexual women in their reports of mental health.

Actually, there were some differences. The lesbians reported themselves to be more independent and self-confident than the straight women. Being happy enough to find that lesbians were not maladjusted, we didn't make too much of their positive attributes, although now I wish that we had. Because we were focused on pathology, we overlooked the positive characteristics and did not include them. It would be decades before lesbians became participants in psychological research and, to my knowledge, still little is known about their positive traits in comparison to straight women.

Perhaps the most notable of the research projects in which I was involved was the development of an internal versus external locus of control scale for children. A reliable assessment instrument was needed to conduct research with children on their beliefs about the origins of control. It would be helpful in investigating various variables such as school success and delay of gratification.

A clinical faculty and friend, Steve Nowicki, came into my office one day and said we should develop such a scale. I agreed and we began the arduous task of selecting items and checking for reliability and validity.

The Nowicki-Strickland Locus of Control Scale for Children was developed and came to be widely used across the world. It was translated into many languages and is still the measure of choice for contemporary research on children's beliefs about internal/external control. Our publication of the scale was also named a Citation Classic.

I was, perhaps, among the first to conduct research with Black children especially in relation to school achievement and levels of aspiration.

As expected, I found career aspirations of the Black children to be of much lower status than comparable white children. Likely, this was because of the role models in their lives who only had opportunities for low-level jobs.

I also looked at delay of gratification among Black students and found them to be less likely to delay than their white counterparts. This study, however, was an example of how unrecognized cultural variables can affect research results.

All of the experimenters who went into schools initially and conducted the experiments were white. They asked students if they wanted a smaller reward at that time or were willing to wait for two weeks to collect an award three times in value.

When we eventually had Black experimenters conduct the experiment, we found the Black student's delay behaviors to be more similar to the white controls. Evidently, a strong variable was the degree to which the children trusted the experimenter to return with the larger reward.

Along with my research and teaching, I continued my clinical work in our psychological center. Additionally, I had a small independent practice seeing about two to three clients a week.

In 1970, I applied to the American Board of Professional Psychology to become a Diplomate in Clinical Psychology. This certification is reserved for experienced psychologists who demonstrate excellence in their clinical work. Requirements were strict, as they still are. I flew to New York to be examined by a group of experts to assess my understanding and knowledge of clinical psychology and its application. I also had to present a work sample and conduct an onsite clinical assessment.

In New York, I went to the Bronx VA hospital to conduct an assessment interview with a client who was until that time unknown to me. He was a young Black male from North Carolina, hospitalized after threatening to shoot passersby from his apartment window.

There I was, a white woman from the South, interviewing a Black male. Moreover, he was catatonic and almost altogether silent during the interview. He did give some limited responses to the assessment instruments and it was easy to determine that he was suffering from schizophrenia. It was far more difficult to elaborate on the dynamics of his background and clinical state. Nonetheless, I passed that part of my examination.

For my work sample, I chose to present a therapy case of a young college male, Dave, whom I had been seeing for about a year. He had come to our clinic presenting a myriad of problems. Dave was deeply depressed and anxious with some psychotic features.

I approached our sessions with a psychodynamic stance; I also saw him in group therapy. As we worked together, he would occasionally talk of his homosexual leanings and how frightened he was of his romantic and sexual feelings toward men.

This was a time, during the early 70s when homosexuality was still a mental illness and a crime. It was certainly not safe for a gay man to be open about his sexuality. I was in a quandary and felt as if I was betraying him by not discussing his homosexual concerns more directly. I did not disclose that I was a lesbian although I know he knew I was sympathetic to his feelings. I was torn in my consideration as to whether or not he should "come out" at that time

Looking back, I know it would have been therapeutic for us to be more open about his homosexual feelings and likely for me to have come out to him. However, we were all so scared back then.

This was another example of my "double life." I really cannot imagine what my experiences would have been like if I could have been open. At that time, homosexuals were castigated as immoral, perverted, sinful, insane and criminal.

How could we live an authentic and open life when these stereotypes doomed us? I simply accepted things as they were. I socialized with my lesbian friends and, concerning the gay life, we only talked of having to be closeted. No one questioned the prevailing climate of discrimination and hate.

In 1969, the Stonewall riots, led by a Black drag queen occurred, but my friends and I never dreamed of rebelling.

In therapy with Dave, we worked primarily on his depression and anxiety. These were, of course, linked to his homosexual feelings to which we had given short shrift. We were successful in reducing his symptoms and he took a junior year abroad in Paris. We exchanged letters and he described how he had become friendly with a young monk, Mike, a counselor in his program. I do not know to what degree they became intimate or if he acted on his homosexuality with other men. I do know that whatever his experiences in Paris, he was a changed person when he returned.

The secretary in the clinic called me in my office one day to say there was a young man who wanted to see me. I asked who he was and she said she didn't know. It was my old client, Dave, who had been through the clinic twice a week the previous year but she did not recognize him. I hardly knew him as well. His hair was to his shoulders and he was dressed in loudly colored bell-bottoms – the penultimate hippie. Dave had left the year before as a fairly buttoned down, conservative college student.

We talked for a short time. He said he was feeling good. We did not see each other again after that. I think I was helpful to him, but I suspect his improvement occurred, not just with the therapy, but more as a result of his relationships in Paris.

I had passed all of the requirements to attain my Diplomate or Board Certification and continued to involve myself in clinical activities.

While on my pre-doctoral internship, I had become familiar with the Gestalt therapist, Fritz Perls. Although originally a psychoanalyst, Perls developed a radical approach that confronted the client with the implications of his or her behavior in the here and now.

Perls was especially attentive to non-verbal cues and used these, plus his own reactions, to engage the client. He often visited Atlanta and I attended many of his workshops. I appreciated his immediate approach and began to incorporate the non-verbal communications of my clients into my understanding of their interpersonal interactions. My therapeutic approach began to be focused less on the past and more on the here and now.

I also came under the influence of Virginia Satir, one of the founders of family therapy. She was a warm, experienced social worker who gave workshops on family therapy across the country and internationally. She too focused on non-verbal communication and developed what would become an influential theory of family work. I felt privileged to come to know her. I learned to see the family as a complex system and incorporated many of her ideas into my own clinical interventions.

Perhaps some of the most important changes in my psychotherapeutic approach occurred through my relationship and interactions with Ruth Cohn. A German Jew by birth, in the mid 1930s Ruth was in Switzerland in therapy with a Jungian analyst. She was frightened by the rise of Hitler, especially when her boyfriend was arrested. While on the couch, she kept thinking that psychoanalysis was never going to change the world one person at a time.

Ruth came to America to escape the Nazis and settled in New York City. A trained psychoanalyst, she began to see clients in therapy and quickly moved to a group approach.

She developed her own theory of group work and established the Workshop Institute for Living/Learning (WILL). Her theory embraced both psychotherapy groups and other groups that might be useful in industry or education, for example.

Ruth believed that a group should have structure and a leader. The time available for the group should be clearly stated and each group session would have a theme. There were certain guidelines such as avoid asking questions, speak for yourself; disturbances take precedence and so on.

Adventures with these new radical therapists were light years away from my early psychotherapy training. Nevertheless, I was always curious about new approaches and anything that would improve my clinical skills. I became very much involved in WILL.

Chapter 19
Civil Rights and Social Action

In 1962, during my beginning year as a faculty member at Emory, I saw my first student demonstration. On the grassy, well-manicured lawn of the campus, a number of well-dressed, white male students, one accompanied by a German Shepherd, were protesting the admission of African-American students to the university. This was in the earliest days of the civil rights movement. It had only been a few years since Rosa Parks refused to give up her seat on a bus. Martin Luther King, Jr. had moved to Atlanta from being an obscure minister in Montgomery, Alabama. The Southern Christian Leadership Conference (SCLC) had been established. All of the schools, restaurants, public transportation, parks, and churches in Atlanta were segregated.

Nevertheless, change was coming. I was lucky enough to be in the heart of the civil rights movement. Interestingly, back then I don't believe that any of us could have predicted that our actions on behalf of Blacks would become a major social movement that changed the country.

The students at Emory were very conservative. Their motto was "Apathy" and they affirmed the Vietnam War. Supported by members of the Johnson administration, secretary of state Dean Rusk came to speak. In addition to rallies on the Emory campus, students held a large rally at the Atlanta stadium. Outside supporters provided funds to fly a large sign over the stadium affirming Vietnam.

Emory students did not seem to be involved in integration efforts. Some of the faculty, however, were quietly going about attempts at desegregation.

A law school faculty, Irwin Levine, had me join Georgians

against Capital Punishment, a group that was well aware that Blacks were being executed disproportionately to whites.

Others invited me to go along with them when they visited faculty in the Black colleges who were quietly working for civil rights. I would go with some of the faculty wives to various restaurants ostensibly for lunch. When we entered the restaurant and asked if they served Blacks, we were always told no. We would then leave the premises saying we could not eat there, leaving the restaurant folks wondering which of us was Black.

My home became somewhat a center for people involved in civil rights activities who needed a place to meet. Most of these folks were students or faculty but there also was a group of monks who joined us. Evidently, they were bound by rules of silence in most situations. But they were talkative at my house planning how they might become more involved in desegregation efforts.

My psychology department chair at Emory and his wife were heavily involved in integration efforts and close to members of SCLC. They knew the major Black civil rights leaders and told them that I, as a clinical psychologist, would like to be helpful.

One evening, about eleven o'clock when I was already asleep, I received a call from Howard Moore, a well-known civil rights attorney. In a genial tone, he asked how I was. Knowing that he was calling beyond a simple conversation, I asked what he wanted. His tone immediately sharpened and he said I must be in the governor's office at nine the next morning. I explained that I needed to go to my job at the university and he responded, "You wouldn't want a man to die because you weren't there."

A Black man, Ernest Whipple, was to be executed the next morning at nine for the murder of a white grocer in Macon, Georgia. He had written a short, poorly spelled letter to Moore pleading for his life. Moore had looked into his case and learned that Whipple was developmentally challenged with an IQ of around 70 or less. Moore needed a psychologist to argue, along with him, that the State of Georgia should not be putting such people to death. Of course, I went to the governor's office. We met with an aide around twenty minutes after nine. Moore explained our reason for being there and the aide called out to someone in another room, "Have they electrocuted that Whipple guy yet?"

Everything was in place for the execution. The warden had called for two physicians. A hearse had arrived and sat waiting. A barber was there to shave Whipple's head. Two telephone lines were open for any last minute calls but the execution had not yet occurred.

The aide told the prison officials to stay the execution for a while. He then listened to us for almost an hour while maintaining that Whipple was guilty and had a fair trial. We argued anxiously on Whipple's behalf.

Finally, the aide talked with the governor who agreed to stay the execution for thirty days. After a new assessment of Whipple's mental status, his execution was commuted. Seven years later, I saw an article in the Atlanta Journal about him along with his picture. He was still on death row but was alive.

I was called on later for yet another intervention. An elderly white man and a number of Black activists were arrested one Sunday morning while attempting to attend services at the all-white First Baptist Church of Atlanta. The group was charged with blasphemy. The only white man in the demonstration was Ashton Jones, an itinerant preacher from Mississippi. He had been traveling through the South demonstrating for civil rights. He claimed he designed the famous picture of a white and black hand clasping each other.

The police who were called to the demonstration determined that if a white man had joined the Black activists then he must be "crazy." Jones was taken to the state psychiatric hospital where he went on a hunger strike. He was then admitted to a general hospital in Atlanta.

SCLC leaders asked if I would assess Jones. They were sure that he was not crazy and hoped I could testify that he should be released. I administered him a battery of psychological tests. He was perfectly sane and I went to court to testify for him. I met several of the other defendants, including Julian Bond and Martin Luther King, Sr.

The courtroom was imposing; the judge stern. The prosecutor was aggressive, attacking my testimony and the assessment data. He maintained that Jones was a communist. Anyone who was a communist in this enlightened country and ran around with Black people must be crazy.

I continued to testify as to Jones' normal mental competence. The judge agreed; Jones was released. The following Sunday he went back to the steps of the First Baptist Church along with several other participants in a demonstration. When police attempted to break up the gathering, Jones bit one of them. This time he went directly to jail.

The Quakers in Atlanta were working along with individuals and organizations for integration. Led by John and June Youngblut, a loose group of folks would come together to discuss strategies for social action. They would also march in various demonstrations. This included volunteers from the North and many Catholic nuns and priests. Authorities from the nun's home order would often contact the Youngbluts to make sure the Sisters were safe.

I never actually marched, but would take my Mustang convertible to the end of a march and transport some of the demonstrators back to the Quaker House. Once this included Phillip Berrigan, an activist priest, who then conducted an underground Mass.

I was privileged to be a part of the group. Using what he could find – bread from the kitchen and water instead of wine – Berrigan began the communion ritual. I laughed with others when he discovered that the clear liquid, which had been on the coffee table in front of him, was actually vodka instead of the water he thought he was using.

The Atlanta police often monitored the activists and marchers. Once June noticed that a young police officer was following her. She pulled into a gas station; he pulled in behind her. She walked to his car, introduced herself, and invited him to join her at the Quaker House. He refused to go to the Quaker House but over the next few weeks continued to follow her. Finally, as June was preparing to march for peace in a Hiroshima Day demonstration, the officer approached her and warned of possible violence. He asked that she not attend the march. To his dismay, she remarked that she would have to march. He then said, "I'll march with you" and he did.

In 1965, after Dr. Martin Luther King, Jr. was awarded the Nobel Peace Prize, Atlanta leaders and some Black and white clergymen wanted to honor him with a dinner. This would be the first time in Atlanta that Black and white people were to sit together at a formal social gathering.

At first, ticket sales were sparse. The idea of a dinner for King was met with opposition from segregationist bankers, merchants and business executives. They feared that their participation in the testimonial would cost them white customers. The Ku Klux Klan threatened to picket the affair. The dinner was almost called off.

The immediate past and present mayors of Atlanta as well as business executives took to the phones to round up support. On the night of the dinner, an audience of almost two thousand split between Blacks and whites, overflowed the Dinkler Plaza Hotel ballroom. The mayor of Atlanta, Ivan Allen, introduced King saying,

"Through the years, as history is wrought, some men are destined to be leaders of humanity and to shape the future course of the world. Dr. King is such a man." Dr. King told the audience that the tragedy of the civil rights movement had been, "the appalling silence and indifference of the good people. Our generation will have to repent not only for the words and acts of the children of darkness, but also for the fears and apathy of the children of light." (Time, February 5, 1965, pg. 24)

My friend, the law school faculty member, Irwin Levine had invited me to go with him to the dinner. We attended and at the close, Irwin asked if I would like to meet Dr. King. We approached the table where King was sitting and still greeting guests. We shook hands and I thanked him for his leadership in the movement. He looked at me with his warm, brown eyes, continued to hold my hand, and said, "No, thank you for all you do." I stood stunned by his compassion, his caring, and his connection with me.

Several years later, after Dr. King's assassination, I had another occasion to go to a large dinner where Coretta King was the honored guest. The banquet included predominantly Black attendees and several husky Black men who stood at the edge of the crowd as if to protect us.

Aretha Franklin sang a number of songs and continued to sing even when the spotlight would go off her. Her microphone was finally disconnected.

A special moment occurred in a speech by Sidney Poitier. He talked of the movement and its future and perhaps for one of the first times in a public gathering, he remarked on "Black Power." There was a sense of urgency in the air. Dr. King had led a non-violent movement, but these dinner guests were obviously considering additional alternatives. The debate as to the tone of the protests was to continue but the tide was beginning to turn. Most folks my age remember where they were when they heard about the assassination of Dr. King. I was attending a regional psychology conference in Roanoke, Virginia. Like others, I was shocked at the news. I felt that I had come to know Dr. King in a special way. I could not believe that he had been killed. I was with Walt Isaac, another Emory faculty member. We joined a somber group who had originally planned a party for that evening. Instead, we were in mourning.

The next day on the drive through rural areas back to Atlanta, we struggled with the car radio to learn of the events occurring across the country. Occasionally, we would hear of violence and of fires. We were especially anxious to know how Atlanta residents were responding. On arriving back on campus, all of us wanted to do something. I helped organize students to be useful during the arrangements for the King funeral.

Some went to the King home to babysit. One of the volunteers, not a student but an older woman – the proverbial little old lady in tennis shoes – answered a phone call that was for Coretta King. Mrs. King said she was busy but would talk when she was free. Later, the volunteer announced with pride that she had kept Lyndon Johnson on hold for 17 minutes.

On the weekend of Dr. King's funeral, Emory men wanted to help and drove their (mostly expensive, exotic) cars to SCLC headquarters. There, they were immediately signed up as members and given cardboard placards to put on their cars.

Can you imagine a new, gull-wing Mercedes with a cardboard sign?

The students then met folks who were arriving for the funeral. One met Bobby Kennedy's family. One picked up four Black men. When he asked where they wanted to go, they said, "Just drive, boy." He drove.

Students were told that they should return to the safety of the Emory campus since "Atlanta's going to burn tonight."

Atlanta actually stayed quiet and the funeral was a serious, sober event. Although they never expected to be members of the SCLC, I have no doubt that many Emory students remember with pride that for some brief, magic, maybe scary moment they were an intimate part of the civil rights movement.

Chapter 20
Dean of Women Days

Having happily settled into my second year at Emory as an assistant professor, I was lying on my living room sofa one evening reading a psychology journal when the phone rang. The voice on the other end was the dean of students, John Robinson. He asked if I knew that the dean of women, a 55-year-old history professor, had resigned to join the Peace Corps. Knowing nothing of the Emory administration, or any academic administration for that matter, I immediately said no. He then asked if I would consider becoming the dean of women, responsible for some 1,200 women students. I knew nothing of what the position entailed, but agreed to talk further with him. My only experience with a dean of women was at my college and I tried to avoid her.

In the fall of 1964, at age 25, I took the position half time and continued my affiliation with the psychology department. I would walk from the psychology building to my new, rather luxurious office in the administration building.

I kept wondering how a kid from the river swamps of northwest Florida and the south side of the steel mills in Birmingham could be in such a lofty position. Not only was I living across the worlds of heterosexuality and homosexuality, I was crossing boundaries of class.

I was moving inexorably into a world of wealthy students and parents, not simply as a professor but as a dean. I was responsible for the safety and security of the women students. I was the advisor for the women's student government and I inherited a sorority system. I held the position for three years until I returned full time to the psychology department.

Working with the women's government was a delight. The female students had their own governance organizations such as the House Council and Panhellenic. Their tasks were to develop policies and procedures for their local group. These then usually went for consideration to the overall Women's Student Organization. I oversaw all aspects of women's governance that consisted of the rules and regulations by which women students abided. Residential house councils and sororities were the major players in proposing and monitoring the governance. Basically, the female students managed their own affairs. I was there to supervise, advise and occasionally become involved in disciplinary matters.

The student leaders were bright and effective. Many looked to me as a role model and decided to pursue graduate or professional degrees. Since Emory had few women faculty and I was the lone female college administrator, I was one of the few successful women they could emulate. I was particularly conscientious, never wanting to fail in their eyes.

As always, I never disclosed my lesbian leanings. No doubt, there were lesbian students, but no one was out. I did come to know one or two senior students and eventually determined that they were lesbians. It may well be that they suspected me, but everyone lived undercover.

Still, I feel very privileged to have been able to relate to and work with so many bright and talented young women. I have continued for many years to stay in touch with some of them and admire their successes.

My very first interactions with the women's government had to do with what I thought were their overly strict early curfews and dress codes, requiring dresses or skirts on campus. No doubt, at that time other colleges – especially in the North – were working on liberalizing such women's regulations. However, I was not aware of their efforts. I felt like I was on my own.

Luckily, I had the support of a thoughtful and activist dean of men. Neither of us could understand why the college men, who were usually the troublemakers, could stay out all hours while the women had to be in the dorms by 11p.m. We worked on getting the restrictions revised to the extent that some of the faculty wives became concerned. They were distressed about this new liberality and complained about me to the college dean. He called me in and, to my great relief, remarked that if folks were not complaining then I would not be doing my job.

Working with the sorority system was extraordinarily difficult. There were very strict regulations about the Rush period that occurred at the beginning of school.

Upper class sorority sisters were not to talk to the entering students during the first couple of weeks. This requirement was to supposedly keep the Rush process impartial. To me, this unfortunate regulation was occurring at a time when students should have been building relationships across classes. First year students should have been learning about what to expect in college.

I worked hard to try to influence sorority members to be more flexible and, finally, the silence requirement was lifted.

I also had more than one student or parent crying in my office because the student had not been accepted into any sorority. My relationship with the sororities and their members was always awkward. I just was not prepared to understand their policies and restrictions. Invited to pour tea at their formal gatherings, I knew I was in the wrong setting.

In addition to working with groups of women students, many individual students would come by my office to discuss problems. One of the more serious was an unwanted pregnancy. This was before the days of easy access to birth control and abortions were illegal.

Along with the women, two Emory men, who had impregnated their girlfriends, also came in to talk. I encouraged them to consult with their partners and their parents to make a decision and come back to me if there were any problems.

My liberal leanings also became a source of concern to some in the community who were members of the John Birch Society, a group of extreme conservative members – mostly Republicans – dedicated to destroying liberals and their values.

My therapist, at the time, knew of the group. He learned that they were hatching a plan to involve me in some scandal that would lead to my being fired. He warned me to be careful and, as far as I know, nothing came of their threats.

Being a young dean of women, likely the youngest in a major university at that time, generated considerable publicity for Emory.

One press release began, "She's attractive, young and knows how to smile."

A newspaper reporter came to interview me and asked about the problems that students would report. I mentioned that not only pregnant women, but their boyfriends as well, would sometimes come to the office to discuss what to do. The reporter had some pictures of me taken and went off to work on a story.

I was stunned to wake up the next morning and see an article with a smiling picture of me on the front page of the Atlanta Journal. Indeed, the article and picture were in newspapers across the country and internationally.

Headlines read, "Young and Pretty Dean of Women Counsels Unwed Fathers."

I kept looking at the picture not believing it was me. I was shocked and confused, with a sense of despair. How could the journalist be so sexist in her writing? The article did not paint a full picture but rather focused on my perhaps unusual experience of seeing a couple of unwed fathers. I could see no redeeming features in the article. The picture was rather a suggestive pose of a beautiful, smiling young woman. I had never considered myself attractive and the picture was very flattering. It was not reality to me. The fluffy story was embarrassing. I was inundated with responses from everywhere. I heard from old friends but most correspondence came from strangers. This included a number of letters from men, including prisoners, who wanted to date me. I had several proposals of marriage, one of which came with an attached phone number.

A man wrote from Alaska and said he was on his way to Atlanta to meet me. I had postcards from him throughout his journey across country. I did meet him in my office and we agreed to go to dinner. Although I felt safe enough with him, our very brief meeting ended abruptly when I learned he was carrying a gun.

Emory officials were pleased with the publicity. A story of how the event came about was published in the campus report. It began:

"The dean's in the limelight. Youth, vitality, attractiveness and unorthodox frankness – plus a German shepherd and a sporty convertible have made Emory's dean of women terrific copy for the press. Too much so, she worries."

All of the attention led to a number of interesting experiences beginning with calls from CBS and requests for comments from other print and broadcast media. I traveled to New York to appear on the television show, To Tell the Truth. I was a local celebrity and sponsor of numerous community activities. Through many weeks and months, I was invited to other colleges and universities

EMORY'S DEAN OF WOMEN

4-E *The Atlanta Journal* Wednesday, Sept. 23, 1964

WAITED TABLES IN DINING HALL

Emory's Dean Young, Pretty

She's attractive, young and knows how to smile. Any of these virtues might be called unseemly, especially if found in Emory University's dean of women.

Dr. Bonnie Ruth Strickland,

the new dean, though is that kind of woman.

SHE IS 27 years old, and found her way to the dean's office through a lot of hard work and sacrifice.

"It was hard work, sure, but

it was also a lot of fun," she said of acquiring her new position.

A rundown of her degrees, papers and honors has already been published. It made a long list.

This story about the dean, is, therefore, a little on the personal side.

"I'm a liberal and a Democrat," she said without being asked.

She gives you her conversa-

tion straight and looks at you while doing it.

HER EYES are big and brown, her hair dark brown, nearly dark enough to be called black.

Dr. Strickland is tan and trim, both attributes gained through swimming and playing tennis.

"I have not married because until now, I've not been located in one place long enough to settle down; and too, the right man hasn't come along," she said. She doesn't go steady, but she does date.

Her life has been busy for a long time.

She worked her way through college waiting tables in the school dining hall.

"Work never hurt anyone, but I see it very fortunate that children have money to attain their education," she said.

As dean at Emory, Dr. Strickland will have about 1,200 coeds in her charge.

HER ADVICE on dating—"I would say routinely, date a lot of people. Perhaps, the best way to go through life would be by coupling marriage with a career."

Dr. Strickland raises German Shepherd dogs as a hobby. One of the dogs is named Garth.

"He (Garth) is a real baby, but he weighs about 110 pounds and who knows, he may come in handy to break up panty raids at Emory," she said.

Staff Photos—Charles Bennett

DEAN STRICKLAND KEEPS TAN, TRIM WITH TENNIS RACQUET: HAS GERMAN DOGS AS HOBBY
Emory University's Dr. Strickland, One of Nation's Youngest College Dean of Women

Coffee honors Emory Dean of Women

Atlanta's Chi Omega's honored Emory University's new Dean of Women Bonnie Strickland (second from right) Wednesday afternoon at Pan-Hellenic House on Clifton Road. Assisting in entertaining are (from left) Mrs. Louis Maloof, president of the Atlanta Chi Omega Alumnae Chapter, serving Miss

Rhea Cravens, president of Emory's Chi Omega chapter, and Mrs. James Simmons, chapter advisor, Dean Strickland, and Mrs. Sanford Atwood, wife of Emory University President Atwood. (Times photo by Grant Zolba)

what fun!

30 *The Atlanta Journal* Wednesday, May 12, 1965

United Press International Photo

WOMAN DRIVER . . . AND DEAN—Dr. Bonnie Strickland, dean of women at Emory University, put on her crash helmet to drive a student-built "car" during Emory's annual student-faculty picnic. Dr. Strickland is one of the nation's youngest women deans, but the distinction didn't help her in the soap box derby which is a traditional part of the annual affair. She lost her race to a political science professor.

SECTION 1   THE COURIER-JOURNAL, LOUISVILLE, KY., TUESDAY MORNING, JUN

Dean Of Women, 27, Hears From The Boys

Associated Press

ATLANTA — One f nation's youngest of women says male students than co to her with their sex p

She is Dr. Bon Strickland, a trim br has brought consid provement to Em sity's campus un often seen driv vertible with a dog draped over

"Unwed stud to me," the who is single view. And her brown e almost no u

How handle h problem

earned her versity. mental collapses among stu ents are caused by mounting pressure. The stu hard for

Dean of Women at 27 Faces Many Unwed Dads

Just a few of the clippings from around the country – Louisville, KY, Tulsa, AZ, and Tampa, FL – highlighting Bonnie's rise to Dean of Women at Emory University in Atlanta, GA.

Unwed Student Fathers Seek Counsel Of Young Dean of Women-Psychologist

By KATHRYN JOHNSON
Associated Press Writer

ATLANTA — One of the nation's youngest deans of women says more male students than co-eds come to her with their sex problems.

She is Dr. Bonnie Ruth Strickland, a slim trim brunette who has brought considerable improvement to Emory University's campus image. She is often seen driving her convertible with a German police dog draped over the back seat.

"An awful lot of unwed student fathers come to me," the attractive 27-year-old dean, who is single, said in an interview. And with a twinkle in her brown eyes she added: "but almost no unwed mothers."

How does Dr. Strickland

DR. STRICKLAND

dean is in charge of 1,600 co-eds at Emory, which has a total enrollment of 5,000. Her youthful outlook helps her in dealing with students of both sexes just about as much as her background as a trained psychologist.

Wearing shorts, a gay blouse and a crash helmet, she recently took part in a campus soapbox derby in which faculty members competed against the students.

Dr. Strickland said she receives many phone calls in the middle of the night from students in trouble of one kind or another. One distraught male student phoned her at 3 o'clock in the morning.

"I'm neither the age of parents nor the age of the students." she said. "And I haven't the remotest idea what

college or quit, marry, get a job and settle down."

students ranges wide, Strikcland said.

"I believe the wides mental collapses amon denis are caused by n ing intellectual pressure student is working too ha his or her ability. There i the growing pressure to graduate school.

"These kids are living most terrifying times. have to grow up too fa Dr. Strickland said sh lieves that campus demo tions are all for the goo "You must remember, said, "that what student trying to do in their d strations is to communic Dr. Strickland was bc Louisville, Ky., and gre in Birmingham, Al; swims, plays tennis and to speak at various programs or give graduation addresses. I appeared on the television shows — *NBC Today, To Tell the Truth* and *The Phil Dunahue Show*. I enjoyed the attention, but always wondered if it was deserved.

When Emory students misbehaved or were in trouble with the police, they were referred to the dean of men or dean of women, almost always the dean of men. Male students caused most of the problems.

I also expect that the administration believed that a man would be more likely to be a strong disciplinarian and had more experience with law enforcement when it was needed – for instance when a student was arrested for driving under the influence. Most of the transgressions were minor, however, (such as underage drinking on campus) and were handled within the college.

The dean of men with whom I had initially worked resigned. He had been at Emory for many years and was simultaneously much respected and feared by the students. After his resignation, another dean of men was hired. I came to know him very well and we enjoyed working together.

Little concerned with disciplinary matters, he brought energy and high spirits to the dean's office. He arranged art shows on the campus and trips to Europe for the students. It turned out he was gay, and unfortunately put the make on the college treasurer's 18 year-old son. When discovered, he was fired immediately. He moved to New York City and took a job as a shoe salesman.

In the absence of a dean of men, I was responsible for all of the student run-ins with the law.

One night, some inebriated Emory men drove their car across the campus lawn and parked under the flagpole on the well-manicured quad. The police were called and apprehended them.

In those days of "in loco parentis," the police, as usual reluctant to refer them to a woman dean, called the dean of the college, a man, and asked him what to do with them.

In stark contrast to prior times when unruly students on campus were disciplined within the college, the college dean told the police that the students should be arrested. The next morning, he came into my office and said we must immediately hire a new dean of men. He was tired of being awakened in the middle of the night.

I knew someone I had met on the dog show circuit, Don, who was leaving a private prep school position. I suggested him for our opening. He was hired and on the job within days. I enjoyed working with him and we have stayed friends since that time.

On one occasion much later, Don came to visit me. We sat with each other and talked of our history together and our professional careers. Even though old friends who had known each other for years, we did not mention the gay life. He was not married and I do not know whether he was gay or not. I did not disclose anything of my being lesbian although he probably knew. Instead, we reminisced about our days at Emory and what twists of fate our lives had taken.

Especially in meeting new people, I have always been concerned about being judged or being safe with them – unsure about how they would feel if they knew I was a lesbian. I likely missed many occasions when I could have been honest about my life and connect with others. I would usually involve myself in an intricate dance to determine if I could be open before I would venture to let them know that I was gay. If there were the least hint that the person would not be supportive, I would quickly change the subject.

I am sure there have been many instances when I could have been more open with others about my life as a lesbian. What a different path my conversations might have taken if I had not been so afraid of being known as a lesbian. I missed authenticity and a depth of intimacy that could have been available to me if I had been more honest. I look back with sadness at the opportunities that were lost to me forever.

Chapter 21
A Psychology Junkie

In 1962, when I completed my Ph.D., it was assumed that one would join the American Psychological Association (APA). So I did. I happily received their publications but was not particularly active. In 1976, however, I answered a call from Dr. Rotter. He was then president of the Division of Clinical Psychology, one of the largest divisions within APA. Dr. Rotter was calling to invite me to become more active in the association. I was surprised and gratified to hear from him. This was the first of my becoming heavily involved in APA. I struggled to meet other members and I kept in touch with them. I joined several divisions and initiated some new programs. I felt at home in APA perhaps because I was a psychologist surrounded by other psychologists. In some ways, I had found my professional niche.

Dr. Rotter gave me my first opportunity to do more in APA than simply read the journals and attend conventions. He asked if I would chair a new committee of the Division on Equal Opportunity and Affirmative Action. The charge of the committee was to recruit and maintain more women psychologists and minorities in APA. At that time, these populations were underrepresented in the division and across the association. I agreed and expanded the charge to include gay men and lesbians.

APA now has some minority psychologists although not nearly enough. Our committee must have done well in regard to women or perhaps we were just in the vanguard of the women's movement. In any case, some 40 years later, around three quarters of our Ph.D. and Psy.D. graduates in psychology are female. Women now make up the majority of members in APA.

The fight for gay rights within psychology and its governance was longer and more difficult. Homosexuality was labeled a mental disorder until 1973 when it was removed from the Diagnostic and Statistical Manual of the American Psychiatric Association. Gay men and lesbians were closeted.

There were, however, attempts to organize the gay community within the association. The Association of Gay and Lesbian Psychologists (AGLP) was formed in the early 1980s.

I received an award from them in 1988 reading:

"In recognition of her outstanding contributions to the welfare of gay men and lesbians."

And, I was delighted when, in the mid-80s, AGLP became a full Division of APA. To be more inclusive, it is now the Society for the Psychological Study of Sexual Orientation and Gender Diversity. I was president of the society from 2009-2011.

Now, the interests and needs of LGBTQ psychologists are openly noted and addressed. APA is a model of LGBTQ rights for other professional associations.

I continued to be active in APA serving on a number of boards and committees and as a council representative. I enjoyed the involvement and getting to know many psychologists. Many knew I was interested in social justice issues. I became somewhat of a role model and mentor to minority and LGBTQ members.

In 1985, I was elected president of the Division of Clinical Psychology, the same division for which Dr. Rotter had been president.

I initiated several new programs and our membership increased. Several folks encouraged me to run for president of APA. My name was known from the various offices I had held in the association and I knew I would be supported by women, LGBTQ folks and minorities. Friends helped me contact APA members to nominate and eventually vote for me.

I failed on my first attempt but came in second. I was disappointed and not certain if I would run again.

Actually, it was not unusual for candidates to run for a second time with increased name recognition from being on a previous ballot. I did run again and on my second try was elected president for 1987.

Now, it is extraordinarily expensive to run for president, but I spent nothing. I was lucky in having some name recognition and the support of many members who knew me.

During my tenure as president, APA was in the midst of a financial crisis. A few years earlier, the association had bought the magazine, Psychology Today. While we were enormously successful with the sales of our professional journals, we did not do well publishing a popular magazine; we lost significant amounts of money.

To stem our financial losses, we sold our buildings in D.C. and Psychology Today. We were then in a position to find a site for a new building and begin its construction. Now, APA owns two buildings in D.C. One – the association's headquarters – is close to Union Station with a magnificent view of the Capitol. The other is close by. One thing APA does very well is real estate.

As president of APA, I represented the association at various meetings, including international conferences, and met with representatives from other mental health organizations. I became friends with my congressional representative, Sylvia Conte. Among other senators and representatives, I met Ted Kennedy and George Mitchell.

In the mid 1980s, I testified in Congress before both House and Senate committees requesting support for graduate clinical programs and funding for the social and behavioral sciences. At the beginning of the AIDS crisis, I was particularly pleased to testify for increased funding for HIV-AIDS research and services.

I walked the halls of Congress marveling about how far I had come from my southern roots. I was happy to be in the midst of APA's advocacy activities and to know I was having some impact on its mission and goals.

There were also humbling moments.

In 1987, I was chairing the APA convention in New York City. As president, I was given the perk of staying in the penthouse of the Marriot in downtown New York. I was half-dressed for a formal dinner when I decided to go out onto the roof. There, by chance, I met the past-president of the association who was without shoes and also barely dressed for the same formal dinner.

We stood on the roof, 42 stories high, looking over Manhattan, and reminisced about how it was that we had ascended to the pinnacle of APA. He talked about his being a half-breed. I talked about growing up to be lesbian. We were both from poor families and raised by single moms. We went to small, unknown colleges and were lucky to be there on scholarships.

Then, we turned to go to our rooms and discovered that we were locked out on the roof. With some chagrin, we pounded on the door and were rescued. We then went to our respective rooms to finish dressing.

The bulk of my time as president was devoted to plans to reorganize the association and restructure the governance.

APA was established with a group of seven meeting at Clark University in 1892. At the time I was president it was a large scientific society and professional association with about 60,000 members. As APA had grown an organizational structure, put in place in 1945, was limited in its attention to the interests and needs of a diverse group of psychologists in the 1980s.

A number of groups and task forces suggested changes, but these were not approved by the membership. The revised plans had almost always been focused on balancing and restructuring a system that would benefit both psychological scientists and practitioners.

Science-oriented members had long been the dominant group in APA but practitioners were increasingly demanding their place in the organizational structure. A proposed reorganization plan was developed to move to a federation model. As president, I chaired the Council of Representatives that approved the new plan and sent it to the membership for a vote. The scientific wing was pleased with the plan and urged its adoption. I was hopeful, too, that the plan would pass. The practitioners, however, felt they were losing their hard won influence in the association and they worked against approval of the reorganization.

In 1987, the plan was defeated by the membership and the psychological scientists decided to establish their own independent society. Thus, the American Psychological Society, now the Association for Psychological Science (APS), came into being. Some members of the newly formed APS remained members of APA but many let their membership lapse.

Organized psychology in this country now had two groups representing it – the larger APA with a professional bent and the smaller APS with a more scientific orientation.

APS is now a healthy thriving international organization with more than 35,000 members, from 80+ countries, and a highly respected stable of scientific psychology journals.

Disappointed in the outcome of the reorganization vote, my involvement in APA and its status quo waned for the next decade. I did spend some time helping with the beginnings of APS. In fact, I was on the ground floor in establishing the organization.

At the beginning, I hosted a small group who wrote the bylaws at my home. I served on its first board of directors. After some number of years, I became re-involved in APA and once again moved into the governance structure.

In 2002, I was elected president of the Division of General Psychology. In 2009, I was elected president of my favorite division, the Society for the Psychological Study of Sexual Orientation and Gender Diversity. Its more than 1,000 members are primarily lesbians, gay men, bisexuals, allies, transgender folks and those identifying with some aspect of being queer or non-binary. I was and am at home in this professional community.

When the president-elect of the division could not become president due to health issues, I served a second term as president. At this time, I was faced with a crisis that not only involved the division but the larger APA as well.

The annual APA convention was to be in San Diego in 2010. Contractual arrangements for convention space and hotels were completed in 2004. The owner of one of the convention hotels, the Manchester Grand Hyatt, had contributed $125,000 to Proposition 8, a law to abolish same-sex marriage in California. Our Division members, as well as others in APA, were very upset on learning that the Hyatt was to be a convention hotel.

It was too late to move the convention to another site. The penalty to APA would have been close to a million dollars and APA was in lean financial times. Many members called for a total boycott of the convention. Factions developed and division members were to choose whether or not to support the boycott. A Work Group, with several division members, and the APA board of directors, was convened to consider the issue. With input from all sides, they worked hard to implement some strategy that would allow the convention to meet.

As president of the division, I was assailed with messages and comments from every side. Many of these were quite vicious with personal attacks and members threatening to resign from APA.

The Work Group and board of directors did come up with a plan. The convention would be in San Diego, but folks were requested not to register at the Hyatt; APA activities were moved to other locations. Buttons were available denouncing Proposition 8 and affirming LGBTQ people. Considerable convention programming was devoted to LGBTQ issues and marriage equality.

The media was alerted to APA's concerns. Many members joined the local on-going boycott of the hotel. We had good attendance at the convention but the Hyatt was dark and shuttered. The crisis had become a teaching moment not only for psychology but also for the general public. Within a few months of the negotiations, the owner gave up his controlling interest in the Grand Hyatt.

I felt like I had helped successfully negotiate the settlement for the division. I felt powerful in my activities and achieved some acclaim. APA and APS have been a strong focus in my life, a bonus on top of my life in academia.

I have enjoyed my time working within both organizations. From the very beginning, I tried to represent the interests and needs of women, minorities and LGBTQ people. Although somewhat out of the mainstream, I still received a number of honors including one of the highest that can be bestowed on a psychologist – the Gold Medal Award for Life Achievement in Psychology in the Public Interest.

Clippings from *The Emory Wheel,* the university's student-run newspaper.

Chapter 22
Therapy

In the mid-1960s, with the breakup of yet another failed relationship, I decided to enter psychotherapy once again.

I began to see a psychiatrist – a psychoanalyst – Steve Castillo, and immediately told him that I was a lesbian. I was enormously relieved when he asked why I thought this was an issue. He did not see homosexuality as a "problem."

We saw each other in what was a successful psychotherapy relationship until he left the Atlanta area. Exiled from Cuba where he had worked in his father's psychiatric hospital, he moved to Miami to be available to the military exiles that opposed Castro.

Castillo referred me to another psychiatrist, Al Miller, who I later learned was also involved with the CIA in regard to the Cuban situation. Miller was a wonderful therapist for me although somewhat unorthodox. For example, he never seemed to start or end his sessions on time. He considered psychotherapy a process of storytelling. Psychotherapy became a process of two people telling stories, listening to stories, and combining both to produce a new story.

In this fashion, Miller often disclosed information about himself, such as his working with the government to provide services for Cuban immigrants. But, I learned later that he had serious heart problems that he had never told me about.

One afternoon, sitting in my office at Emory I received a call. "Is this Dr. Strickland?" they asked. I replied that it was. They then said, "Do you have an appointment with Dr. Miller on Friday at 2 o'clock?" I replied that I did. The voice on the other end said perhaps you have not heard, but he died of a heart attack (at age forty-four) while on vacation. I was devastated.

I immediately began to search for another therapist. I called Castillo in Miami and we talked of Miller's death. Miller had been a consulting psychiatrist in a private psychiatric hospital close to Atlanta.

Castillo remarked as how Miller carried a small bottle of ammonia with him. When he saw hysterical patients, he would whip out the ammonia and have them smell it. He would then remark that this would help them. It actually worked for some people.

Castillo then said he knew that Miller had died. He could not explain it but he was sitting with his father in the family living room when he had a strong sense of the smell of ammonia. He even got up to look around but found nothing. He knew of Miller's heart problems and knew then that he had passed away. This revelation was from a strong scientist type who was not prone to paranormal events.

Castillo reminded me that he had previously referred other therapists for me. I opted for Sidney Isenberg, another psychiatrist.

At my first meeting with him, I asked, "You're not going to die on me, are you?" He replied that he might.

Isenberg was also an exceptional therapist for me. We continued in the vein of the work I had done with Miller. Although he was psychodynamic in his therapeutic style, I don't believe we talked much about my family or my early experiences. We focused more on my relationships and breakups. We saw each other for a couple of years until I left Atlanta. I later learned that he was gay.

A short while after I moved to Massachusetts, I found a health care provider. I was alone in my home one evening. The phone rang and a voice asked, "Do you have an appointment with Dr. McIntosh tomorrow at 10?" My heart sank, my stomach churned and all the old feelings of panic around Miller's death flooded over me. The voice then said, "We're just calling to confirm."

A few years after I moved from Atlanta to Massachusetts, I began to feel very irritable. I was less careful about my dress and found myself continually arguing with people. On one occasion, I went to my bank to talk of some sort of mistake I thought they had made in my account. After the discussion, I walked through the bank with the impulsive urge to toss the furniture around.

I knew that something was wrong and I drove myself to my health care provider. When escorted into the examining room, I was agitated and lay down on the floor. The nurse practitioner I saw immediately referred me to psychiatry.

I saw a therapist there for several years. One of the most important things she said to me, after my mother called imploring me to do something about her lost dog (I was 1,500 miles away), was "Your mother can very well take care of herself."

I was also introduced to my medicine woman, a psychiatrist and expert in psychopharmacology. We have been doctor/patient for more than thirty years and she still prescribes medications for me.

I have continued in psychotherapy up until the present, seeing the same therapist for some twenty-five years. I go in now mostly for tune ups every month or so. She is an experienced therapist and a lovely person. I feel enormously grateful for her compassion and care.

My mood swings have diminished. My anxieties and obsessive-compulsive behaviors are reduced. This improvement may also be the result of medications that I take. Sometimes, I miss the old episodes of hypomania. Mostly, however, I feel balanced and emotionally stable.

Chapter 23

A Double Life

My foray into heterosexuality continued through my early years in Atlanta. I lived a double life. In fact, it may have been a triple life in that I was also an imposter from the working class in a privileged environment.

In my posing as a heterosexual woman, I would present myself as a young professor who dated men. On the other hand, I was usually romantically involved with a woman. She and I would talk about our background and experiences and move carefully into a relationship.

My life was very different when dating men. We were much more superficial in our conversations and in our relationship with each other. Living deep in the closet was painful but I thought necessary. If "outed," I would have been immediately fired.

It would be years before I could bring myself to look more closely into the effects of living a closeted life. I am sure I still do not fully understand the consequences. I have to believe though that I have been wounded and scarred – always fearful of being "found out."

Likely, the reasons that shaped me as a lesbian are complex and occurred early. Growing up I thought that I must assume a stance of being perfect, trying to assuage my mother's punitive responses to me. I tried to anticipate how my behavior might affect her.

I still plan ahead, often for weeks, preparing lessons, lectures, and presentations. I keep my car filled with gas. I check to make sure I am not forgetting anything. I hate to be late to anything; someone might disapprove. I pay my bills early, obey all traffic rules, and do everything in my power not to be found wanting in any way. Possibly, this has to do with my early inordinate anxiety when faced with the possibility of being "found out" for some infraction.

Although I consider myself now mostly open about my lifestyle, I still find myself cautious. A few years ago, I had some gay material open on my coffee table when my plumber arrived to fix a leaky pipe. I immediately hid it, unwilling to let a stranger know I was a lesbian.

I feel comfortable now in my being a lesbian although I am still cautious. If there is no reason to bring up the subject, I don't. Mostly with new people or groups, I stay quiet.

Interestingly, when I teach I usually disclose to the students that I am a lesbian. In my last class, however, I introduced myself with a somewhat lengthy description but failed to mention that I was gay. Being more comfortable in my life style, it just didn't cross my mind that it was an issue.

At Emory, I could never talk about my lesbian relationships with my straight friends or my colleagues at work. I was very close to the male faculty in my department. We bowled in a league together and, after a long while, they invited me to join them in their weekly poker game. They may have been curious about my home life, but they never asked personal questions.

I was fortunate to know one faculty member in our clinical program who was gay. We became friends and would occasionally go with each other to social gatherings pretending to be a straight couple. For department parties, when he was not available, I would show up with another handsome, charming man on my arm. Little did my faculty friends know that all my dates were gay.

Shortly before I left Emory, the chair of the psychology department had a small going away dinner party for me and invited my close faculty friends. I arrived with a handsome gay man and people's attention quickly turned to him. They asked where he had gone to school, what he did for a living and more. A graduate of Wharton School of Business and in retail, my friends soon recognized him as the son of the owner of a large major department store in downtown Atlanta. The next morning the chair called me in to tell me he was very impressed by my date. He and his wife thought very highly of him; he wished us all the best.

After leaving Joyce and my first home in Atlanta, I moved into an apartment complex that had a number of lesbians as residents. This was my first introduction to the gay community in Atlanta. I only stayed in the apartment for a few months because I was eager to have my own home once again.

As it turned out, my "little sister," Jane, from college lost her teaching job in Florida. She had become involved with a fifteen-year-old female high school student. Jane moved to Atlanta and took over the apartment. I bought a house and moved into my second home, this time by myself.

I also bought several lots in a beach community not far from Dalkeith. I would eventually sell those lots and buy a beachfront second home in Mexico Beach, Florida.

Having my own home became enormously important to me. I realize now that I have always been trying to make a warm and safe place for myself. I want to be independent and self-sufficient, relying on no one else, immune to the influence of another.

I would be the hostess, the one who would invite others in. I also realize now that in my past relationships, I tried to be the nurturer, the caretaker. Only in my later years have I begun to relax and, with some trepidation, let others take care of me. Nurturing and protecting the other became my style of interacting with women.

I also had any number of friends stay with me in my home as had my mother when I was growing up. Once, when Jane came for a visit she stayed a year and a half.

Although during the time that I was there, Atlanta had a substantial lesbian population, it was still not easy to find other lesbians. There were two bars in town that catered to white lesbians. I assume there were meeting places for Black lesbians, but in our completely segregated city, I never knew of them. The two white bars seemed to differ according to social class. A downtown bar in a rough section of town attracted working class women, usually from the factories. They often dressed as men and were accompanied by feminine companions. The patrons of the second bar were more likely to be teachers, nurses, or office workers. I heard that the bars stayed in business through payoffs to organized crime.

Another venue of engagement was women's sports. Lesbians organized and played in softball and basketball leagues and came to know each other. The most frequent way of meeting others, however, was through private parties in people's homes.

These were never safe and, if known about, were frequently raided by the police. The police routinely collected license plate numbers of cars parked near the bars or the private parties giving them a list of lesbian participants as a way of knowing who they were. I was fearful of going to the bars, including the men's gay bars, though I did meet other lesbians through social gatherings and the softball and basketball teams.

As I gradually came to know lesbians in Atlanta, I began to date. I was especially attracted to vivacious, charismatic, beautiful women. I would become involved with these women, but they would invariably leave me. I would then retreat to a safe affair with a steadier and maybe not so beautiful woman who would never leave me. Then, I would get bored and leave her.

This pattern continued for many years. I do not know why this slot rattling, but I was likely reacting to the rejection and then the boredom. My two long-term relationships were with women who were a combination of these traits. One was to last for 18 years and I am still with my second partner of twenty-three years. My relationship with my mother had softened somewhat. I would occasionally go to Birmingham to visit. I know she was proud of me, but we never talked about personal matters. She was still trying to find men for me to marry and we never discussed that I was a lesbian.

I also reconnected with my brother, Bud. He had completed college on a full tennis scholarship and then went to dental school. In college, he met a lovely young woman from a relatively well-off family from South Carolina. Her father was a state senator and she a debutante. She and Bud eventually married and he established a dental practice in South Carolina. Theirs was a storybook marriage with two delightful daughters.

My mother and I would usually spend Christmas with Bud's family as the girls were growing up. My nieces are now with solid, special men and my youngest niece has two children. Even though my mother passed away, I still spend Christmas with Bud's family and watch my grandniece and grandnephew grow up.

Chapter 24
Living with Lovers

During the 1960s, I dated any number of women. The first after my breakup with Joyce was a woman a bit younger than me. We saw each other for about a year and a half. We enjoyed being with each other and liked doing the same things. However, she was just beginning graduate school in psychology; I was settled professionally. Our lives were in different spheres. We eventually separated.

A male hairdresser friend, knowing that I was single, mentioned a cute, sparkling young woman, Beth, who had just broken up with her partner. I invited her to come by for drinks at my home sometime. She did, indeed, appear. We had wonderful times together. Beth introduced me to a number of her lesbian friends, including her aunt. They were all professional women, with a preponderance of physicians.

While we were together, Beth, who had been working for a nonprofit organization, decided to go to graduate school in psychology. Expelled from her undergraduate college when the administration learned that she was gay, she returned and graduated after making up her requirements. A gay faculty friend helped her be admitted into his graduate program. Beth eventually received her doctorate in school psychology and began a practice in Atlanta.

We were together for almost three years until I fell in love with a therapist from New York. We had met at a psychology group workshop in New England and immediately began to make trips between Atlanta and New York to be with each other.

Beth did not take the impending separation lightly. She threatened suicide and I tried to refer her to a well-known therapist that I knew. He returned my call late one evening. I answered the phone with a sleepy voice and he asked if I had been drinking. I had not. John Warkington was a famous psychiatrist very much sought after for treatment by other psychotherapists.

I had come to know him through professional conferences. I recall once when I heard him speak, he said that the most important thing in life is loving and hating significant others. I am still not sure I understand the hating part, but I know John based his therapeutic approach on clients being able to enter an open and honest relationship with him. He was always alert to any disruptions in the therapeutic alliance including when the patient was drinking.

I told John my partner was threatening suicide. He immediately asked her age. I told him she was in her thirties and he said, oh, he probably couldn't be of help. He believed that anyone over fifteen who truly wanted to commit suicide would do so. He did agree to see her, however, and she kept a few appointments.

She also determined that instead of killing herself she would kill me. She left a note on my Emory office door written in blood, "You cannot love so I cannot live."

I knew she was angry and disappointed with me, but I had been unaware of her deep rage. Now, realizing how serious she was, I was scared.

Beth took to prowling the campus in our Mustang convertible looking for me and saying she had a gun. One Friday, I was looking up material in the Emory medical school library. I decided to call the department staff before I returned to my office. They said that Beth was waiting for me in the hall. I asked to speak to one of the faculty and talked to a friend, John. I told him of my situation and asked if we might meet off campus for lunch.

John and I met. I told him that my partner was angry and threatening to hurt me. I was afraid to go home. He invited me to his home with his wife and kids for the weekend. This created quite a stir in his suburban neighborhood. All of a sudden, a new, young woman was hanging out with John and his family at the neighborhood pool. Neighbors kept asking about the nature of our relationship wanting to believe that I was a sister or cousin. When the weekend was over, I was still afraid to go home. I spent the next few days with my college friend, Ginger, who had given me the intelligence tests, at her home on the outskirts of Atlanta. Eventually, things with Beth cooled down. I left the New York therapist and although our romantic relationship ended, Beth and I eventually became friends again. She became a well-known child psychologist with her own radio and television shows and an overly full practice.

Sometime later, I was at a lesbian softball game in a public park when I ran into Jane, my "little sister" from college. Sitting in the bleachers was a handsome, beautifully dressed woman with salt and pepper hair, almost completely silver. I asked Jane about her.

"Everybody knows Nell." she said.

It turns out, she was a popular high school physical education teacher who was a winning basketball coach. Not only did she take her girls to many a state tournament and win but she also helped coach the boys' team.

I was not to meet Nell in person until a few years later. We were both at a party at Jane's. We began talking and Jane came over to us. She pushed us together and said she wanted her favorite two people to be friends.

Shortly thereafter, Nell and I met again when some friends planned a lesbian tennis tournament. The organizers purchased some tee shirts with H.O.T.T emblazoned on them. When one of the players went to pick them up, the sales clerk asked what the initials stood for. Unwilling to tell him the real meaning, Homosexuals Only Tennis Tournament, she quickly answered Hell of a

Tennis Tournament.

We put on the t-shirts and, by luck, I was matched with Nell as a doubles partner. We won the tournament. I was eager to see more of her, called her and we began to date.

At the beginning, I was more serious than she was about the relationship and we both continued to date other people. I called her one night and asked if she wanted to go with me to a basketball game in which I was playing. She declined and I learned later that she was hoping to go out that night with another woman. When that date did not materialize, Nell decided to come to the ballgame. In the meantime, I had asked another woman I was dating to go with me. Nell arrived at the ball game, saw the other woman in the stands, and quickly learned that she had come with me. Nell was not happy, but she didn't say anything at the time. However, after that, we started to see each other exclusively.

The courtship was a rocky one, but we were determined to make a go of it. Nell had recently broken up with a country and western singer and was still mourning that relationship. They had been together for some five exciting years. Nell traveled with her as she performed across the country and in Europe.

After some number of months of dating, Nell moved in with me. She had a small, chocolate toy poodle, Sugar, and I had my shepherd, Pak. We were happy in Atlanta. Nell had a wide range of friends who embraced me.

Emory's salaries were stagnant and I pursued other positions. Nell was ambivalent about my decision to leave Emory after I had an offer from the University of Massachusetts (UMass). We had only been together for about a year or so but wanted a longtime relationship.

I moved in 1973 and after a year of indecision, Nell moved north as well. I had bought a house in the woods that had been in the process of being built. Nell joined me in our new home. We were in a rural community that was only about fifteen minutes from the university. The house was an unusual and interesting contemporary. We both liked it.

Nell and I settled into a somewhat traditional marriage style; my earning the living and her being the proverbial homemaker. We were welcomed into the community and played together in a women's, mostly lesbian, feminist softball league. We came to know many lesbians in liberal western Massachusetts and enjoyed a rich social life. Welcomed by the faculty and administration at UMass, we were treated like any straight couple.

Nell did not work, but took care of the house and the meals. We would often get into arguments about something or the other, but, generally, life was okay. We traveled extensively and particularly enjoyed international trips. We also spent time back in Atlanta visiting with friends and family.

We particularly enjoyed playing in a feminist softball league (which may be an oxymoron). It was begun to provide opportunities for women of all skills to play in an inviting and leisurely game. If a batter thought the pitcher was pitching too hard, she could ask the pitcher to slow down. The league was begun with team names such as The Incorrects, New Attitude and Red Hot Lovers.

In explaining the rules to the new players, our coach mentioned that the outfielders should call the ball if it came close to them. One of the new members remarked that she felt that to be too much of a commitment. A few of us on the team, in rebellion and tired of the constant adaptations of processing our every move, called ourselves the PIGS – the Politically Incorrect Girls Softballers. We wanted to be competitive and against the new rules; for example, we decided we would bring beer to the games. Our team, the Common Womon would occasionally hold mock homecomings with our arch rival, the Hot Flashes. We had a majorette who would parade around in a skimpy costume. Petite and attractive, she would hurl her baton high toward the sky, exposing the dark hair in her armpit.

Nell and I lived in that home for eleven years. The dogs, Sugar and Pak, passed away but we enjoyed a new dog, a chocolate Labrador named Pace. We tried to breed Pace, but she had only one puppy that we gave to friends in Atlanta. In our attempt to find a male stud for Pace, we had met a realtor who had a male chocolate lab. There was a lake just three miles from our home. I often fished there with a graduate student, Bill Haley, and told the realtor that I would be interested in seeing any properties that came on the market along the lake.

Several months later, the realtor called to say that an old, lakeside farmhouse on two acres of land was available. I immediately made an offer that was refused. A year later, the realtor came back to say that if I was still interested, the owner would accept my first bid. I bought the farmhouse, refurbished it, and rented it out during the school year. Nell and I would spend the summers at the lake.

On one cold February Tuesday in 1984, the contractor, Henry, who had worked on the house and I walked up the long driveway toward the road. He looked back and said, "What a spot for a contemporary." I asked him if we might move the farmhouse to another site on the property and build what we wanted. He remarked, "Not now. I just finished the renovation with new framing and new windows. Not now."

The following Friday morning, I called Henry to tell him that we could move the house. It had burned down the night before. Electric tape covering an exposed pipe had shorted out and started a fire that destroyed the house. The renters who were staying there at the time had escaped the blaze and no one was hurt. Henry was then free to build a lovely new contemporary house; Nell and I moved in.

As our life together continued, Nell and I began to spend more time apart. Our dog, Pace, was having laryngeal spasms. Nell spent time with Pace while she was being treated at the University of Georgia Veterinary School. I stayed in Massachusetts. We gradually began to drift apart. Nell seemed to be relatively happy in the relationship although we were fighting a lot. On the other hand, I was less satisfied. I was increasingly caught up in my teaching, research and my activities in APA. Nell remained the homemaker.

After 18 years, I told Nell that I wanted us to separate. She was hurt and disappointed but moved to our beach house in Mexico Beach. There she was healthy and happy, busy socializing and playing bridge. Surrounded by friends, she was active and well-loved in the small community. I maintained the home for her and saw her often until Hurricane Michael hit in October 2018.

I watched with trepidation as weather reports broadcast the arrival of the hurricane. Mexico Beach had been through many such storms before, some damaging, some not so much. Thinking that this was a typical storm, Nell evacuated with a day's change of clothes, her heart medicine, and, luckily, her lock box containing important papers. Turns out, the key target of the Category 5 hurricane was Mexico Beach. The house was completely swept away, leaving only a concrete slab. The loss of the house was a traumatic event for Nell and me. We lost everything, but I received a generous insurance settlement and still have the beachfront lot.

After Nell and I broke up, I began dating a number of different women. I have a veritable Army of ex-lovers although I have lost contact with most. I am still in touch with a few, especially those who I was with for a long time or whose relationship was especially meaningful for me.

In the mid-80s, as I was turning 50, I met Diana when I was

visiting the university in Boulder, Colorado to give a talk. She had never been romantically involved with a woman, but we were instantly attracted to each other. Although two thousand miles and two time zones separated us, we entered into a romantic relationship. She would visit me in Massachusetts and I would spend the summers in Boulder.

Diana was a psychologist in private practice. She had called me before my visit to say that she hoped we might meet while I was in Boulder. She mentioned her name and I looked down at a publication on my desk. She was the author of a paper on violence against women, one of the first to be published in that area.

I was instantly intrigued since the whole movement about women and violence was just beginning. I had just sponsored a symposium on the subject, which included Linda Fairstein, an attorney in New York City who had begun one of the first legal programs assisting women victims of violence. She is now a popular author.

Diana attended my talk in Boulder and we met for supper following the program. She invited me back to her home in the mountains. We talked for hours.

She had been married for 17 years but had no children. Following her divorce, she was single for a few years and always exclusively dated men. Her life was busy in that her therapy practice was full and she was an adjunct instructor at the University of Colorado. In her leisure time, she ran marathons, competed in triathlons, and was a long distance bicyclist.

I returned to my lodging way after hours, but Diana and I had made plans for us to meet again sometime before I left. We did meet, exchanged phone numbers, and vowed to be in touch. We then supported the telephone company with our long distance calls and airlines through our many flights to see each other.

We were together for some two to three glorious years. Life

with Diana was exciting and glamorous. She was a fashion plate who dressed me, as well, in stylish clothes I had never worn before. We traveled extensively, always staying in boutique hotels. We went to the Santa Fe Opera, attended the Telluride Film Festival mingling with movie stars and directors. In her late model convertible, we often traveled to Vail where she had a condominium. We skied and enjoyed après-ski on the mountain. She introduced me to friends from both Vail and Boulder and we had a rich social life.

However, there were dark spots as well. Diana always seemed jealous and suspicious if I spent time with others. One time, she stormed out of an after ski gathering accusing me of attending to the others at her expense. Another time when I was at breakfast with a friend, Diana appeared uninvited and unexpectedly joined us. Once, on driving back from the mountains on a cold winter day, we stopped for gas. Diana was cleaning off the windshield. From inside I pointed out a spot she had missed. She angrily got back in the car saying that this was the most humiliating thing that had ever happened to her. Surprised, I could not quite believe that.

One of our final fights was a time she accused me of possibly becoming violent with her, something I had never dreamed of. She also accused me of coming on to a new woman friend that she had met. She seemed determined to be in control, manipulating each situation to be the center of attention. We tried couples therapy with Diana choosing one of the best-known and most respected therapist in Denver (Diana would only go to the best).

We went to two sessions with me doing most of the talking. After the second appointment, Diana declared the therapist incompetent and we never returned. No doubt, I had my faults in the relationship, but I began to realize that I could never adore Diana enough.

We separated and for the first few years after our breakup, we

Chapter 25
A Sad Journey

One day, some ten years after we broke up, I called Diana just to catch up and she remarked that her news was not good. The leukemia had reoccurred. She met with her physician who offered her the choice of a sixth round of chemotherapy or the decision to withhold treatment. Knowing the treatment would not be a cure, Diana decided against it. She was given three to six months to live.

I was stunned. I sat in frozen anxiety while panic swept over me. Some nine months earlier, I had gone through the death of a long time gay male friend with whom I was very close. I had comforted his surviving partner of more than forty years, spending two weeks with him.

Losing close friends was clearly on my mind. I did not know what to say to Diana or how to respond. I finally asked if there was anything, I could do. She answered, "Come to see me." I stumbled at a response, saying that was not likely. I had just returned to a busy schedule at school and probably could not make the trip.

I immediately told my longtime and current partner, Marjorie, about the conversation. She announced, "Of course you're going to go."

I looked through my schedule to see when I was most free and found a time some three weeks later. I called Diana back and told her I was coming. She seemed delighted but puzzled as to why I had changed my mind. We agreed on the dates of a weekend coming up. I booked tickets to Denver and a shuttle to her home in Boulder.

Preparing for the trip was difficult. I kept thinking of what it would be like to see Diana, of how she was feeling, and what the weekend of my stay would be like. I agitated over packing, changing the clothes I would pack from moment to moment. I am always a little anxious when I take a trip. In fact, I am often anxious when I start out on my daily routines. What if I forget something? I have a list of things, glasses, hearing aids, keys, and so on that I often review when I am starting out. This trip was particularly anxiety inducing. I checked and rechecked reservations, tickets, and the gas in the car.

I drove to the airport worried that some disaster would occur on the way. I was not worried about running out of gas. After all, I had checked the tank many times. However, I was afraid the car would break down or I would have a wreck.

I tried all the anxiety-reducing techniques I knew, relaxation, deep breathing, and being in the moment.

I heard a strange noise from the car on the passenger side and became even more distressed. About two thirds of the way through the trip, however, I noticed that the passenger side front window was slightly open. I closed it and the noise disappeared. My anxiety did not, however, but I chalked it up to the impending visit.

After having started out way earlier than I needed to, I parked and took a shuttle to the airport. I arrived to find long lines and learned that my flight through Chicago had been cancelled. There had been a fire in a control tower that serviced O'Hare and Midway rendering travel in and out of those airports impossible. The agents were rebooking passengers on the following day. I was not going to fly the long distance for only one night in Boulder and resigned myself to having to find another time to travel. When I got to the agent, however, he was able to book me on a non-stop flight later in the afternoon. My spirits soared. I recovered my car and drove home for the few hours that I had.

My return trip to the airport was uneventful. My anxiety was much reduced. After all, I had worried about all the wrong things and I had a practice run. The flight left on time and I arrived just a few hours later than my initial arrival time.

An airport shuttle took me to Diana's condominium and I rang the bell. She buzzed me in and I looked up the stairs to see her smiling. She was stunning, her hair having grown back after she was bald from her treatments. She was dressed like a model that she had once been. She appeared in good shape physically although she had trouble catching her breath after the least exertion. We embraced and commenced the weekend.

I marveled at the beauty of Diana's downtown condominium that she had moved into after selling her mountain home. It was small, contemporary, tastefully decorated and with one bedroom. Windows soared for two stories. White furniture in the living room sat on a black and white rug. There were touches of red throughout the space on pillows and in the original contemporary art on the wall.

Diana always prided herself on her decorating taste and her condominium was beautiful. In the next morning light, however, I looked out the window over a busy street and saw a gas station and car wash across the way. It was sad for me to see. This shabby scene was in such stark contrast to her beautiful indoor space and the old surroundings of her former mountain home

It was late and we did not talk much but rather went to bed early – me on the sofa in her living room.

We were up early the next morning and lapsed into our old familiar routine of her preparing breakfast. Diana squeezed fresh orange juice, always a breakfast ritual, and cooked eggs and sausage. She had always prided herself on being an excellent cook. This time, however, the sausage was raw as was the chicken that she later barbecued for supper.

Another unusual behavior was her failure to remember for us to have lunch. She also repeated herself many times over the weekend. I was dismayed by the behavioral disintegration and her memory loss.

After breakfast, we settled in to talk about her leukemia and her prognosis. I was not surprised that in her usual fashion, Diana had scheduled every moment of my visit. She laid out the plans and I readily agreed. It was something of a relief that she was in control.

We discussed the details of her health and how she planned to spend her last days. Upon learning of her three to six months to live, she had contemplated suicide, giving her a last chance at control regarding the timing of her death. Talking with her palliative team, however, she had decided against it although I was not clear what her reasoning had been.

Diana was alternately reasonable or crying. She was extremely emotionally labile. While she had always been good at expressing positive feelings, she had always been reticent about anger or anything negative. Now she raged against the leukemia going from extreme despair to an optimistic air of trying to make the best of things. I did not know how to respond except to listen and let her know I was hearing her.

In late morning, we went to the Boulder Farmer's Market, always an enjoyable pleasure for Diana. She knew many of the vendors and exchanged words with them. She seemed connected to them in ways more than being an acquaintance. She smiled and spoke to complete strangers. I felt she desperately needed to be in touch, to have human contact however superficial.

After forgetting to have lunch, Diana lay on her bed in her bedroom. I sat beside her feeling helpless with her hand on my arm. She talked of how she had been so optimistic about recovery during her five hospitalizations; how she felt so sure that she would beat the leukemia. She spoke of her disbelief that it had re-occurred. She asked if I believed in an afterlife and cried through her deepest fears of dying. She talked of how afraid she was, especially that her late symptoms would be painful and she would not know how to cope. She would then recover from her tears somewhat and talk of how she wanted to spend her last days engaged in those activities that brought her pleasure. She reassured herself that she had good friends who would be with her, but talked of the anger she felt toward her two sisters from whom she was estranged. I listened, sometimes also with tears, wondering how I could comfort her.

I had lost close friends before and thought of what would have happened if we had actually lived together. Even if I had moved to Boulder, I believe we would have broken up. If we had actually made a go of it, I would now be alone without her. All sorts of thoughts ran through my mind. Who would be with her at the end? How could she survive the inexorable journey toward death?

Sunday morning, a bright Colorado one, Diana and I took a walk and then drove into the mountains to see the aspens in their full glory. The day was gorgeous. It was hard to be sad in the beauty of the fall foliage. The brilliant yellow of the aspens was highlighted against the deep green of the ponderosa pines. I knew that Diana was thinking about this being the last time she would see the fall and the change of seasons.

She was, though, looking forward to her upcoming birthday in November when she would turn 75. She planned to invite friends to a party at her home and calmly discussed how many people her small condominium could hold.

All through our visit, an unclear nagging thought had been nipping at my brain. As I prepared to leave, the thought became clear. I would return to my beloved. Diana had no constant companion, no partner, and no significant other. There was no one to be with her, to take walks, to share meals, to sit comfortably and quietly with, to wipe her tears, or hold her close in sleep. It was not my place any longer and perhaps she was not in the dire need that I would have felt not having someone. I asked what she was going to do after I left and she said she would probably read.

During my weekend with Diana, I was of two minds. I wanted to leave, to escape the strain, the walking on eggshells, afraid that I would do or say the wrong thing. At the same time, I wanted to stay, spend time with her and savor each moment. I was still torn when the shuttle arrived and it was time for me to leave. Diana walked with me down to the street. We said goodbye and embraced for the last time. She died a few months later.

Chapter 26
Health and Illness

It was a glorious vacation in Greece during the summer of 1976. Traveling with Nell, we had first a week in Athens staying with friends who were spending a sabbatical there. I had met Dick and Joan when I was on sabbatical at the University of Hawaii (where my only continuing education was scuba diving).

Dick was on the faculty and welcomed me to the university. We often had lunch together and he introduced me to what was then, for me, exotic food from Korea and Vietnam. I became so enchanted with Hawaii that I toyed with the idea of staying there. At a psychology departmental Fourth of July party, we all got a little drunk. The department chair offered me a position in early infancy. I accepted on the spot. The next day we all sobered up. Since I had absolutely no knowledge or interest in infants, the department chair was mightily relieved when I declined the offer.

One day, Dick said that he could not go to lunch. He and Joan were going to a park where they would receive their adopted baby son. Later they were to adopt a baby girl. I still stay in touch with Dick and Joan, visiting them in Hawaii just a few years ago. Dick retired as a dean at the university while Joan continues to work as a photographer. One of her prints hangs in every room of the Sheraton Hotel on Waikiki Beach. Matt and Maile and their families live in Oregon (Maile with grown up twin sons) having left Hawaii which they found too limiting and too expensive.

When we were in Greece, the children were young and Nell and I loved being with the family. We roamed their neighborhood, sampled local foods, and enjoyed homemade wines. Maile, who was about two or three, had long blonde hair. When we were out, she was a marvel to the dark haired Greeks who gathered around to admire her. Complete strangers would approach as we walked through the streets. We met and talked to many folks that we would not have known otherwise.

When we were not with the family, Nell and I visited the museums and marveled at the antiquities. We rambled through the bustling marketplace, laughed, and joshed with merchants as they pushed trinkets and souvenirs on us. In the calm of the night, we watched the moonrise over the Acropolis.

We spent the second week with Dick, Joan, and the children visiting the Greek islands. We stayed a few days on Kos, hiking the hills and eating octopus on the beachfront. We admired the Aesceplion, where Hippocrates is credited with building one of the world's first hospitals on a beautiful site overlooking the Aegean Sea. Patients would come there to a place with no stress. They would be well fed and cared for, take hot baths, and talk to physicians. We then visited Patmos where St. John is said to have written the Book of Revelations. We saw other sun swept islands, their colorful houses jutting out to the sea.

For the third week, Nell and I left our friends and went to Crete. We sunned on white sand beaches, wandered through the Mycenaean ruins, and wondered at the glories that are Greece.

Back on the mainland, we went on a land tour into the Peloponnese and saw Delphi, the alleged center of the universe. It was there that my universe shifted and another journey began. I started to hemorrhage vaginally.

For many years, I had a heavy menstrual flow and the spring before the trip a D & C. All seemed well at that time but now I was gushing blood. The tour guide could not find a physician but referred me to a local veterinarian. He came to my room, gave me a shot, and in broken English kept repeating – abortion, abortion? This was certainly not the case, but I was relieved that the blood flow was somewhat staunched.

Late the next day we arrived in Naplion, a small seaside city. When I went to bed, I lay on my back feeling as though my body was shutting down. I felt strangely calm and thought back to my home in Massachusetts. I contemplated the thought that I was dying and envisioned myself lying on my deck at home in the sunshine with my dog beside me licking my face.

I awoke the next morning to learn the tour guide had located an English-speaking ob-gyn doctor. I sat in his rather dingy waiting room surrounded by pregnant Greek women. When he examined me, he seemed disturbed and said, "You have lost a lot of blood," an event, of course, of which I was well aware. He gave me a shot and some iron in small glass vials to take with me. He pondered as to whether I should have a blood transfusion but rather urged me to return home, which I was scheduled to do in the next few days.

When I came home, although the bleeding had stopped, I immediately saw my regular ob-gyn doctor, Schifrin. He tossed the glass vials into the wastebasket saying you will cut your hand when you break them and you do not need to lose any more blood. He gave me iron in a more accessible form. He also said that I was fortunate that I did not have a blood transfusion in that it could have been contaminated with all sorts of unhealthy debris.

Two months later, I was sitting in my psychology office when I began to hemorrhage yet again. I immediately went to my medical group. Since Schifrin was not available, a new physician examined me. He said he hated to interrupt my day but said I had to go to the hospital. There, I underwent another D & C.

The phone call came from a nurse. She said that the surgeon wanted to see me and asked if I could come in the next day. Alarmed, I asked her what he wanted to see me about. I knew the news would not be good. She said the doctor would talk to me tomorrow. On the next day, I went to see him. He said that a biopsy had found irregular tissue from my D & C and we should schedule an appointment for a hysterectomy. It looked as if I had uterine cancer. When I began to look at my calendar, he said we should schedule it as soon as possible.

I went back to my office after the visit with the doctor and could not get the possible diagnosis out of my mind. A close faculty friend came in and I told him of the situation. He was sympathetic and shared with me that his sister had cancer. Somehow, this was not very reassuring.

I went in for an appointment with Schifrin. He was in clear agreement with the surgeon. Moreover, he reassured me that my surgeon was excellent. He said that if his wife needed this kind of operation, he would encourage her to go to him. Schifrin added that he would see me as soon as the surgery was completed.

I don't recall feeling afraid. However, one afternoon I was sitting in my living room thinking about the fact that I had cancer. A wave of anxiety swept over me. I realized for the first time that I might not survive.

I talked to a few other people about the cancer and especially Nell, my partner at that time. She was very supportive although she was, perhaps, more frightened than me. She did everything for me and gathered with friends at the hospital for the surgery. I was relieved of my teaching responsibilities. All of the faculty who knew about the cancer were exceedingly sympathetic and understanding as was my department chair.

The operation went well. The day after surgery, Schifrin stopped by the hospital. Having been on a trip, he came to visit on his way home from the airport. This was in early November during the presidential campaign of 1976. Schifrin must have been a Republican and worried about socialized medicine under a democratic president. He said he was happy that the surgery was scheduled on Election Day when I was in the hospital and could not vote for Jimmy Carter. Being a good southerner, an ex-Georgian, and a Democrat, I cheerfully announced that I had voted absentee for Carter.

Schifrin told me that I had been lucky. Uterine cancer often goes undetected because there are few if any symptoms. My bleeding, while scary at the time, had essentially saved my life. It had enabled me to get care before the cancer had spread or become more dangerous.

According to the biopsy, it looked as if the cancer was both sarcoma and carcinoma. Schifrin said that this was not likely since these two cancers seldom occurred together. However, the cancerous tissue was sent to a tumor clinic and, indeed, the results came back that it was both.

I had a friend who was on the faculty of the Veterinary School at the University of Georgia. She had long been engaged in a number of studies on viruses in chickens and especially to what degree they were related to cancerous tumors. She said she would love to see the carcinoma/sarcoma tissue if it could be made available to her. I talked to Schifrin and the tissue was sent to her. As far as I know, I am famous in the veterinary school chicken virus archives at the University of Georgia.

My general physician had followed my case, prepared to assist me with any further treatment. She contacted physicians at both Bay State Medical Hospital in Springfield and Massachusetts General in Boston for their recommendations. Mass General wrote back that because the cancer had likely trickled through the vaginal canal that I should have a radium implant to destroy any lingering cancerous tissue. Bay State recommended no further treatment.

About this time, my general practitioner disappeared. I learned later that she was admitted into a residential drug treatment facility. Other physicians took over my case and somehow the Mass

General recommendation was overlooked. Turns out that was a stroke of luck as I later learned that the radium implant might likely have spread the sarcoma.

I wondered a lot as to the causes of uterine cancer. Some suggest that estrogen may be implicated. When I was in graduate school, during the late 1950s to early 1960s, I had a bout of heavy bleeding. I went to the Health Service at Ohio State. A physician prescribed me birth control pills that she thought might regulate and diminish the bleeding. These were the very early days of the birth control pills and contained substantial amounts of estrogen.

Many years later, in the very late 1990s, I was being treated for depression. My psychiatrist added estrogen to my drug regimen having had some success prescribing it for depressed patients. I was surprised at its effects. I felt better. All of a sudden, I found myself looking at men with a new eye, gauging their attractiveness. I began to buy dresses. I am still amazed that a drug can so influence one's perceptions and behavior.

The complexity of the degree to which estrogen can be implicated in regard to cancer of the reproductive organs is still being investigated. For me, after two years of being on estrogen, (which may or may not have been the cause), a radiologist, looking over my routine mammogram, found suspicious signs in my right breast. I went to a hospital for a biopsy. The attendants put a small medal wire in my breast, the one identified with suspicious cells. I felt altogether silly, sitting in a hospital clinic with a wire in my breast. I was in a waiting room filled with well-dressed women – so different from the time in Greece.

Again, I made my way home. I stopped by a liquor store, perhaps subconsciously needing a drink. By chance, the clerk, Tony Kramer, had been a student in one of my classes. He asked how I was and I blurted out the situation. He was particularly sympathetic trying to reassure me that things would turn out all right.

My disclosure began a new relationship with Tony and I saw him several times after that. My shopping for additional liquor was probably not as great a need as my wanting to have some contact with a new friend. We stayed in touch through the years. I attended his wedding and we still correspond.

The physicians found evidence of intraductal carcinoma in situ and performed a lumpectomy. I assumed that would be the end of it. Unfortunately, the margins around the site of the cancer were not clean. Another lumpectomy was performed. Again, the margins were not clean.

This was getting serious. At this point, I had little left of my right breast. The only remaining treatment was a mastectomy. Having never been especially attached to my breasts, I was not particularly alarmed about the loss of one of them.

Looking back, I am amazed that the whole event seemed so ordinary. I was never frightened and had no fleeting or even continuing anxiety. Friends were supportive and Nell amazing in her love and concern for me.

My surgeon this time, Nancy Weiss, was a very well respected older woman, esteemed by her colleagues. As I was lying in a room before going into surgery, I looked up to see a handsome man, obviously a physician, lean over me. It was my old ob-gyn doctor, Schifrin. I had not seen him for some twenty-five years between cancer surgeries, yet he recognized me. He asked what I was there for and I told him, intraductal carcinoma in situ. He immediately said that is the best kind of cancer to have and told me I had the best surgeon as well.

Once I knew I would be having a mastectomy, I was curious about what kind of reconstructive surgery might be suitable. Surprisingly, while I had an oncologist, a surgeon, and my general practitioner, we never discussed the benefits or drawbacks of surgery replacement or reconstruction. I knew there were several alternatives available including doing nothing, a prosthetic, a silicon implant and a trans-flap procedure.

I talked with friends. One, who had once been a model, said, "Don't, by any means, choose a prosthesis or a false breast." She remarked that she had a friend with a breast prosthesis, who was playing golf one day. Her friend hit a long drive and the ball sailed straight down the fairway along with the prosthesis.

After a mastectomy, a simple procedure is to do nothing. A scar remains and one is flat-chested where there once was a breast. Most women, however, want to rebuild the shape and look of the lost breast. Especially when one is wearing a bra or a swimsuit, it is nice to be balanced across one's chest. Silicone implants were a choice although at that time there were concerns about leaking. I became more and more enamored of a trans-flap procedure, especially in that for me it came along with a tummy tuck. I liked the idea of using my own muscle to replace the lost tissue. I was not aware, however, of what a major procedure this was. The plastic surgeon cuts into the skin of the stomach area right below the lost breast. He or she then removes muscle tissue and relocates it in the lost breast area. The muscle tissue is shaped into a breast and firmly implanted in the chest. The procedure takes some time to heal. One may sometimes suffer back pains later as the body tries to regain its balance. A second surgery is required to shape a nipple and tattoo an aureole. Still, I opted for the trans-flap procedure.

When I came home from the hospital following the surgery, I was in a manic state. I would sit up well into the night emailing friends about what had been happening. One friend, Ted, an old graduate student, wrote back that he was delighted to hear that the surgeon managed to get the new breast on the correct side and properly aligned with pre-existing structures. I had also mentioned in my voluminous emails that I was going to have to talk to my department chair as to whether I might have the spring semester off since I still needed a nipple tattoo.

Ted wrote me back with some advice as to the strategy with which to approach her.

"First, expunge the word 'tattoo' from your vocabulary. It invokes too many images of Harley-Davidsons and black leather."

Another email correspondent said she would like to see me on a Harley in black leather.

Ted continued, "I haven't completely formulated the jargon yet, but a brief sentence or two should suffice – as long as the words "surgical," "post-operative," and "reconstruction" are used liberally. Perhaps even something along the lines of "targeted mammary re-focalization" (i.e., putting the bulls-eye back on the boobie.) And, I was just wondering. When your new breast itches, do you scratch your stomach? Does spicy food lead to sexual arousal?"

I still have a massive scar across my stomach from the transflap procedure and I am a bit lop-sided. Still my new breast looks natural. Both breasts match; both sag. However, I need another tummy tuck.

While I consider myself relatively healthy, I am fraying at the edges and feel signs of aging creeping up on me. Being a two-time cancer survivor, I am on anxious alert to every ache and pain I feel. I need glasses and hearing aids. The hearing loss is my greatest disability, isolating me in social situations where I cannot hear, embarrassed to ask people to repeat themselves. I sleep with a machine to reduce sleep apnea. I have a benign tremor, at least I hope it's benign. I am a walking pharmacy for medications for blood pressure, cholesterol, diabetes, bipolar disorder and other ailments. My joints are creaky. Stairs are higher and distances longer.

Chapter 27
Transition Time

In 1973, Nell was a high school teacher and noted basketball coach. She had been teaching for sixteen years and was making a good salary for that time. In fact, she was making almost as much as I was with a Ph.D. and eleven years of university teaching. Salaries at Emory were low. There was little hope of having them improve unless one received an offer from another school.

One day the clinical faculty went out to lunch instead of holding a regularly scheduled meeting. We had pizza and beer and for the first time reported our salaries to each other.

As Emory was a private school, faculty salaries were not public information. My salary was among the lowest. Having had perhaps too much beer, we returned to the campus and accosted the department chair. He said he would ask the college deans to come and talk to us about salaries. Indeed, the graduate school dean and the college dean did meet with us. They said they would try to provide more information.

After a few weeks, the college dean returned and said, "You asked me a question. Will faculty salaries improve? The answer is No."

He explained that the endowments that supported Emory, mainly from Coca Cola, were targeted to medicine and nursing. Moreover, the elderly major benefactor had no major heirs. Emory stood to receive a substantial endowment at his demise but nothing was going to change in the near future. Several of us then decided to look for other positions, not necessarily because we wanted to leave. We needed an offer from another institution that Emory might match.

Immediately prior to this time, I had taken my first sabbatical at the University of Hawaii. I truly enjoyed the relaxed atmosphere, the beautiful weather, and the quick friendships that developed. The Hawaii experience led me to believe that other universities might be as inviting, if not more so, as Emory. I began to think seriously about applying elsewhere.

We were always looking for funding for graduate students. I had a particularly exceptional student, Dan Hale, who I hoped to support. Visitors from the National Science Foundation came to Emory to discuss research-funding opportunities. I went to a meeting with them. A tall figure stood up across the room and came over to me. Norm Watt was a fellow classmate from graduate school. We had an immediate reunion. Wanting to spend some time with him, I took him to the airport. He had been at Harvard in the psychology department for several years and then moved to the University of Massachusetts in Amherst (UMass). I asked if he knew of any employment opportunities. He said his department routinely kept a listing of possibilities mostly at small colleges in Massachusetts. He said he would send me the list and asked me to send him my curricular vita.

I had done well at Emory. I had published extensively. My teaching evaluations were excellent. I was named an Outstanding Professor. I was promoted to Associate Professor in a timely manner and had tenure. I had external funding through a research grant from the National Science Foundation. Within a very few days after he received my curricular vita, Norm called to say there was an opening at UMass and invited me to apply. However, by the time I visited the campus, the position had been awarded to another psychologist.

That made the interview process much less stressful for me. I was very relaxed during my presentation and in meeting the faculty and students. I was also somewhat relieved that I would not be living in New England.

As it turned out, however, the other psychologist declined the offer and in 1973, I was offered the position at UMass as a full professor in the department of psychology with an excellent salary.

I conveyed this offer to my department chair at Emory. He immediately said they would do what they could to keep me. I was to be promoted and my salary increased although not to the level of the UMass offer.

I was torn. I had a rich network of friends in Atlanta. Nell did not want to move. I was not thrilled about living in the North. However, UMass offered considerably more support and resources than Emory.

I talked to one of my senior colleagues, a well-known child psychologist. He encouraged me to take the offer, saying that at Emory I would always be the young assistant professor. I would be starting anew as a senior figure at UMass.

I had worked with this particular faculty member on the research on gay and lesbian mental health. With a wife and family, he was passing as straight although I learned later that he was a gay man. Sadly, a year or so after I left Emory, at the end of one semester, he prepared his grades and then went home and killed himself.

Conflicted about the decision, I went back and forth between what to do about staying in Atlanta and moving north. I had spent four years in Ohio, a foreign culture to me. I did not look forward to going back north. I was not even quite sure where Massachusetts was.

On my plane trip there for the visit I was not surprised that we flew over New York City because I expected Massachusetts to be only slightly south of Canada and the Arctic Circle. I knew this would be truly Yankee country.

Yet, the UMass offer was so extravagant in my eyes that I

would be foolish to turn it down. I could take my favorite graduate student with me and he would receive full funding. One faculty friend noted that with my increase in salary I could afford to fly back to Atlanta as often as I wished.

I made my decision to accept the offer from UMass and prepared yet again for a move north. Some scenes remain vivid in your memory no matter how many years pass. I recall with such clarity pulling out of the driveway of my Atlanta home and pointing the car north, afraid, in what turned out to be the case that I would never live in the South again.

I often returned to Atlanta and to Emory to visit. I would spend time with friends and I loved seeing my old faculty buddies. I missed them terribly. I know I could have been happy in Atlanta if I had stayed. However, I also recognized that my life at UMass was much enhanced. Professionally, I flourished with wonderful graduate students, a continued involvement in research that I enjoyed and that brought some acclaim, deep involvement in my psychology associations, and my continued love of teaching. Personally, I began to relax in being an out lesbian.

I have even come to appreciate living in Massachusetts, the most liberal state in the country. I have new friends, a lovely home on a lake and I met my current partner, Marjorie, with whom I have lived for almost twenty-five years.

Chapter 28

From Home to Home

When I pulled out of my driveway in Atlanta to leave for Amherst, in the summer of 1973, I looked back at the house I had lived in for almost a decade. There were shrubs grown tall from when I first planted them. The brick wall I had built by the side of the carport was still standing straight and true. Someone else would now mow the always too-large lawn.

Even though I had the beachfront home in Mexico Beach that I visited often, I would be leaving it all far behind. My feelings were sweet and sad.

I remembered the good times of sharing my home with friends and partners. The entertaining, the socializing, the parties, the quiet times alone. I had sat in my living room watching the cataclysmic events of the decade of the 60s unfold – the Cuban Missile crisis, the war in Vietnam, the assassinations of King and Kennedy. I had watched with horror the killing of college students at Kent State. For me, this was too close to home and the students I saw every day.

I reflected on my time at Emory as professor and dean and thought about the sabbatical that allowed me the confidence to think about leaving the South. I recalled my involvement in the civil rights and women's movement. I wish I had done more. Most of the reflections were pleasant and happy. I tried to forget the hard times, the disappointments, and the breakups that had thrown me into despair and left me sobbing alone.

I wondered how I could leave my colleagues, old lovers, and the comfort of being immersed in a warm community of friends and lesbians. My family was in the South. How would I see them as often being so far away?

I had always lived in a southern culture. I knew my history, growing up in the segregated South trying to overcome assumptions about people different from me. I knew I would have to work at moving past my prejudices against Yankees – against everyone who was not from the Deep South. I thought about the world I was about to enter.

I had attended high school and graduate school and moved to Atlanta knowing no one. In Massachusetts, I did have a friend and his family from graduate school days. A bright, wonderful graduate student who I knew well was accompanying me. I had made my choice to move.

I went to Amherst to look for housing, but did not find anything I wanted to buy. Not wanting to rent even for a short time, I bought a condominium but looked forward to the excitement and challenge of continuing to search for my permanent home.

I enjoyed the prospect of moving to a more rural area beyond the bustle of Atlanta that was becoming more crime-ridden and snarled with traffic. I was supervising a graduate student at Emory when he received the word that his girlfriend, an undergraduate at Emory I knew, had been brutally murdered in their apartment a few blocks from campus. I knew I would not miss the dark side of Atlanta.

Of course, I wondered about my new position at a large research university so different from the small college atmosphere I had enjoyed at Emory.

Emory was rather parochial. Most Emory students came from affluent backgrounds and were preparing themselves for professional careers.

On the other hand, I knew UMass to be a "people's university" with a large number of first-generation college students. UMass students had protested in great numbers against the Vietnam War while Emory students had affirmed the war.

I thought about the large classes of students I would teach, the increased pressure of doing research, and how I might relate to my new colleagues. I wondered how it would be to live as a lesbian in a new, liberal community.

My move was life changing; I was not at all certain that I had made the right choice. Does anyone feel confident about a major decision, which for me was both a move and a professional change? I was anxious about leaving all I knew with a bit of tingling excitement about new adventures.

One of my most desperate concerns was whether my then partner, Nell, and I would continue to be together. She had urged me to seek other job possibilities so that I might improve my salary at Emory. However, she never believed that I would actually accept an offer that would take me away from Atlanta and from her. She was at first unwilling to move with me although she entertained the idea that she might eventually join me, which she did.

During the first fall semester while living in the condominium, I looked at houses across the area. I hoped to be somewhat close to the university but also in a country setting a bit isolated from neighbors. I wanted natural space around me and a home with lots of light.

During the summer, I saw a site overlooking a pond with lots of natural beauty where a house was to be built in Belchertown. By fall, it was well under construction. A contemporary, it seemed perfect for me and I could pick out wall colors, appliances, and so on. I decided to rent or sell the condominium and buy the house. I had trouble finding a mortgage since banks were uneasy about lending to a single woman. But, I was able to purchase the house at the turn of the year. I loved it.

After a year, Nell joined me and we were there for eleven years until we built a house on a lake only three miles away.

Chapter 29

Teaching

Since I had always wanted to be a schoolteacher, I loved living in the academy. I was doing all that I ever wanted to do, reading, writing and talking to people. In addition to my teaching responsibilities, I had a part-time independent practice seeing a few people for psychotherapy. I had also worked in the Psychological Services Centers at Emory and at UMass teaching clinical courses, supervising students in their clinical work, and running therapy groups. I enjoyed the clinical work, especially the supervision, but my great joy was teaching.

Through the years, my teaching changed dramatically. At first, I lectured in every class and gave examinations that covered the material. Perhaps this was necessary in the large classes I was teaching. As I came to teach smaller classes, I began to lean more heavily on student discussions. Psychology, in which we are curious about behavior, especially our own, is an easy topic for people to pursue.

Now, I am no longer the only teacher in the room. Every member of the class has something to teach and each of us has something to learn. I continually encourage the students to share their questions, their experiences and their answers to other people's questions. I want students to be in the here and now and make the most of our time together. I want them to be cooperative and not competitive, to share ideas, and help one another.

When I was playing in a feminist softball league, one of our mottos was "Every mistake helps another woman." Every mistake in class gives students an opportunity to explain and help. No question is too trivial; no statement unimportant.

I assume that everyone in the class wants to do the best that she or he can. My job as a teacher is to make this happen. Everyone has something to offer if given the opportunity to express themselves. Not only do students learn from each other, but they will also learn they have something of value to offer. None of us has to be the expert. When we need to be exposed to some specific topic about which we know little, I simply ask a real expert to come and talk to the class. The students and I all learn something. I have a notion that we learn best when we link new knowledge to old information and to ourselves. Experiential learning is deep and lasting.

A returning graduate student, who had been out of school for a dozen years, recalled an exercise from a family therapy class that I once taught. I had asked him to be a part of a family structure in which one marital partner dominates the other. To illustrate, I had him kneel and put his foot on my shoulder.

I asked how we would resolve this dilemma of domination. He looked rather stricken but then I simply stood up. He toppled over. The returning student, now a professional psychologist, said that lesson was one that had stayed with him more vividly than anything else he had learned in the class. It was not only an example of family dynamics, but also a lesson for everyday life.

In one of my favorite classes, I try to teach assessment and treatment of various mental and emotional disorders. Students are to become familiar with current psychotherapies.

One day in class I mentioned how anxious I was to make a scholarly presentation in a seminar I was taking. The students immediately launched into a psychotherapeutic intervention, namely cognitive behavior therapy.

They demanded to know what evidence I had that the presentation would not be a success. Had I ever given a "bad" lecture before? How often? What was the likelihood that I would be a failure? What would be the consequences if I was not brilliant?

They gloried in their newfound expertise in providing psychotherapy and my anxiety was much reduced. The presentation went fine.

Finally, I try to provide a safe space where confidentiality is maintained. Students know that they share only what they wish. I try to build trust. Often this is risky because we are usually so guarded about ourselves, fearful that others will not like us if they get to know us.

Yet, I know that sharing our history, our hopes and our dreams, allows us to enter into more intimate interactions with others and gives us a renewed sense of our humanness. Further, we recognize and own our deepest feelings of authenticity when we are regarded unconditionally.

I try to have every student in the class know that she or he is important and valued. In building trust, we build empathy and understanding that, hopefully, allows us to be open to learning.

Chapter 30

Faculty Life, Administration and Failed Retirement

Life at UMass was quite different from my time at Emory. My classes ranged from 300-500 students and there were new preparations. Luckily, I had a number of graduate teaching assistants to help, supplemented by some undergraduates.

We would often meet in my home so I was quickly involved in interactions with small groups of students. I also attracted wonderful graduate students. Their research and scholarship was impressive and many have gone on to become respected and acclaimed psychologists.

One proposed a theory of feminist liberation. One teaches residents to have faith-based church and synagogue participants monitor and advise other members about health issues. Another was among the first to investigate stress among caregivers. One is dean of a nursing school.

I am proud of all of my students and pleased to know that most, whatever their professional careers, have involved themselves in social advocacy. Their efforts toward social justice and their concerns with disadvantaged groups, brings me special pride.

A friend of mine, Doris Abramson, wrote a poem with the lines, "Would the pupils come back, please, to tell who I am by telling me who I was to them once."

One of my greatest joys is hearing from old students and learning about their lives, especially their involvement for the social good. On one occasion, on a trip to an undergraduate advisor's conference, one of my colleagues mentioned that the department needed to add a new course, maybe health psychology. She asked if I would be willing to teach it. I declined but out of nowhere offered to teach a course on something like Lesbian Studies. The chair asked me to write a course description and submit it to the faculty senate Curriculum Committee for approval.

Well, you would have thought I had offered to endow a building. The Senate Committee enthusiastically approved the course and voted it in unanimously. I began to teach Individual Differences: Explorations in Lesbian Psychology. In the early 1980s, this was among the first offerings of its kind in the country. The students took their learning beyond the classroom, organizing teach-ins and demonstrations on behalf of gay rights.

I was not long at UMass when I became involved in administration. My second year there I became graduate director for my department. In my third year, I became chair. My teaching and research may have suffered but generally, I enjoyed administrative responsibilities. I learned that one of the wives of one of our older faculty members was perhaps the lowest paid full professor in the university. I was especially pleased to remedy this situation. I also became involved with the university's Status of Women committee trying to be of help to women who came to the committee as victims of discrimination.

The school song for the university still reflected the all-male student beginnings. I railed against the administrators until they relented and changed some of the words of the song from "Sons of old Massachusetts, devoted sons and true" to "Sons of old Massachusetts, devoted daughters true."

UMass had been a leader in recruiting women to faculty positions but still had a way to go to support women and treat them equally to men. As chair of the psychology department, I also chaired our executive committee which included seven area heads (clinical, experimental, etc.), a student representative, and other administrative department faculty. Much of our meeting time was spent trying to recall how we used to do things. I persuaded the group to vote on a policies and procedure manual, outlining our current organizational status. Having this allowed us to quickly look up our policies and procedures and put new ones into place. I also persuaded the area heads to combine their areas from seven to four. These actions seemed to be helpful and remain in place with the merging and development of some new areas.

Much of the work was routine, chairing the personnel committee charged with promotions, approving faculty hires, preparing a budget, meeting with other chairs and the dean, etc. My time was filled but I also wanted departmental members, faculty, staff and students to enjoy themselves.

I planned a number of social events. Once we had a party in a space on campus but were not invited to return. Another time, we held a party off campus at a local athletic facility. The police closed that one down. Our departmental members knew how to party and have a good time.

I also launched a pseudo-athletic program for the department. Faculty and students – mostly graduate ones – came together to form various sports teams to play in the university intramurals. Another faculty member and I won the mixed doubles tennis championship. We also fielded a co-ed volleyball team that won its bracket.

Perhaps our greatest adventure was our women's touch football team with male cheerleaders. We had skill practice in one of our building's seminar rooms. Perhaps we should have had more physical practice on the field. We never won a game. We thought we had a chance when we learned we were to play a sorority. Turns out it was an athletic sorority. We lost by a landslide. In fact, as I recall our record for the season was 0-7. Our average points per game were something like minus 2.

Toward the end of my second three-year term as chair of the department, I received a call from our new chancellor, Joe Duffey. He had been politically active in Washington and barely lost in a run for the United States Senate from Connecticut. Joe invited me to the chancellor's home where I met with him and his wife, Anne Wexler.

Anne was a strong Democratic political operative who founded the first major Washington lobbying firm headed by a woman. She was one of the capital's most influential lobbyists and a key inside player in Democratic politics. Anne helped prepare Geraldine Ferraro for her vice presidential debates, served on the Rules Committee of the Democratic Party, and eventually on the transition teams of presidents Carter and Clinton.

At the chancellor's home, Joe invited me to become his associate in the chancellor's office. I do not believe either one of us knew what this entailed, but I accepted. I moved into a nicely appointed office next to him in the administration building. He was a delight to work with. A kind and gentle man, he was a superb administrator.

As Associate to the Chancellor, I was basically a troubleshooter when problems arose and a stand in for Joe when he was away. I followed him around the campus sometimes trying to put out fires that were occasionally of his making.

A generous man, he could not say "no" and kept giving up desirable and limited space to different groups. I had to explain to disappointed departments and units that they could not really have the space that he had already delegated to others.

I attended meetings with Joe and sometimes represented him. Many of the meetings were ordinary, such as the faculty senate, but others were of a more glamorous nature. I met with the board of trustees and legislators and became involved in university administration at the highest levels. I was traveling in heady circles.

I loved being at the center of power in the university. Joe was routinely on the phone with Washington politicians. I remember one time when a presidential hopeful called, Joe had me answer the phone and say he was not available to support him being already committed to someone else. Another time, Joe invited the Dalai Lama to campus and arranged for me to be on a program with him.

On one occasion, Joe realized that I would be in Washington over a weekend that Anne would be there. He arranged for me to meet her for brunch at an upscale restaurant in DC known for catering to politicians. I was in Washington for a business meeting of the APA and told some of the staff about my upcoming brunch.

They looked at me in dismay immediately saying, "You must dress up and in no way can you wear those fur lined leather gloves." We cobbled together something from my limited wardrobe and what they loaned me.

When I arrived at the restaurant, I found that Anne had two guests. One was Sheila Tobias who had just published What Kinds of Guns are They Buying for your Butter? The other was Meg Greenfield, a prominent columnist for Newsweek.

The topic of conversation was whether the military should move to smaller units that could engage the enemy more easily than larger battalions. I had nothing to say on the subject. As had happened so many other times, I found myself in the company of famous people wondering how I got there. I was living beyond my wildest dreams and enjoying every moment.

Anne Wexler was important in my life in another way as well. A prestigious appointment came up for the National Institute for Mental Health Advisory Board. Although Reagan was president, Anne worked with her Republican counterparts and I was appointed to the board. We oversaw all mental health grant proposals that came into the Institute. When there was a vacancy for a new director, we were a decisive body in selecting him. It was always a "him" back then.

I enjoyed my time working with Joe. I liked being in the midst of things. I liked knowing what was going on at every level of the university and being at the center of important decisions. I thought about remaining in administration at UMass after Joe left the university.

I was nominated for a UMass dean's position but was not selected. I considered some administrative positions at other colleges and universities, but either I did not get the job or I did not accept the offer.

In what turned out to be one of the most important life decisions for me, I returned to my faculty position and reemerged myself in scholarly activities. Having passed on administrative offers from other institutions, I was able to remain in my home in Massachusetts, stay involved with my community of friends, and pursue my first love – teaching.

I continued my teaching and research for almost fifty years at UMass. In 2002, the university offered a buy back depending on one's age and number of years of service. I thought about it for a while and decided to take the offer. My pension was only slightly less than my faculty salary and I would be relieved of department meetings and committee work.

When I took the buyout offer, I assumed I would involve myself in the usual retirement activities. I took up golf (I hated it) and immersed myself in numerous volunteer opportunities.

I was not particularly happy though. In one instance, as a member of my local historical society, I was recording names and inscriptions from the gravestones in one of our cemeteries. It was a cold November day with snow spitting from the sky. My fingers were numb and I could hardly write. I gave up, deciding that this task was more suitable for the Boy Scouts.

Other volunteer activities were more ordinary. I led discussion groups at assisted living facilities; I helped in a local survival center. I even spent a short time in local politics being a representative to a community governance group. I continued my involvement with APA, which I enjoyed.

Mostly, I found that I was, and am, happiest when I'm teaching. Luckily, I was able to continue to teach small undergraduate classes in the Honors College, albeit part-time, at UMass. I am able to design my own seminars, which have become popular offerings with high ratings; my classes are always oversubscribed.

Obviously, I flunked typical retirement, but I'm no longer just filling my days with an abundant of community projects. When I'm not teaching, I remain busy with activities that I truly enjoy.

I play tennis two or three times a week, mostly with other seniors, some into their nineties. We do not always remember the score or who is serving, but our spinning drop shots leave our opponents flatfooted with eyes glazed over. We cheer our good shots and whine at the bad ones. I have also taken up pickleball.

I joined a Learning in Retirement group that offers a variety of peer-led seminars ranging from Wine Tasting to Economics 101. I generally take one or two seminars each semester and have moderated a couple.

Mostly, however, I enjoy being a schoolteacher and the fact that I have lived my life in the academy. I have been enthusiastically returning to school every fall since first grade – almost eighty years ago.

220 Leaving the Confederate Closet

Chapter 31
Late Family Life

While I sometimes miss the South and the warmth of its people, I am happy living in the Pioneer Valley of Massachusetts. I live on a lake in Belchertown, a town adjacent to Amherst. In my home, art objects and collectibles from travels all over the world surround me. I feel blessed to be in such lovely surroundings both indoors and outdoors.

Mostly, I feel blessed to be with a partner of almost twenty-five years. I met Marjorie at a party in Connecticut. She was (and still is) beautiful, charming and a delight to be with.

She was leaving a marriage of twenty-three years and I was solidly single, although dating. At the party, we talked and learned that we lived within ten minutes of each other in Massachusetts. I was determined to see her again and was able to reconnect to her through friends.

Born in 1949, Marjorie was the first child in her family followed by three brothers. Her mother had come from some means, but her family lived modestly on a farm in rural eastern Massachusetts. They ran a dog kennel. Surrounded by many animals, Marjorie especially loved her ponies.

Marjorie's parents divorced and she moved with her mother to western Massachusetts. Her mom had a job caring for laboratory animals at a private women's college, Mount Holyoke.

Marjorie completed high school, went to secretarial school for two years and then traveled on her own through Europe and the Mideast. When she returned to the states, she considered being a midwife and learned of The Farm in Tennessee. An intentional community, The Farm was self-sustaining and then had about six hundred residents. A number of women came to The Farm to train as midwives. However, this training was restricted to women who had given birth. Since this was not the case for Marjorie, she became a teacher on The Farm instead.

People on The Farm were devoted to good works and developed a program called Plenty to reach out to those in need. When earthquakes in the 1970s devastated Guatemala, Plenty was mobilized to help restore the villages and damaged homes.

By this time, Marjorie had met and married her husband, and the two of them went to Guatemala as part of the group providing relief efforts. They stayed for three years before returning to the states because of the widespread violence in the Guatemala countryside. They brought with them their first son, a Guatemalan baby, who, at twelve days, had been abandoned with sepsis in a hospital.

Wanting to be close to her mother, Marjorie and family moved back to Massachusetts. The couple lived with Marjorie's mother and a second son was born. Marjorie occasionally taught part-time, but was basically a stay-at-home mom.

When the children became older, Marjorie went to Mount Holyoke and graduated Phi Beta Kappa, magna cum laude. She then went on to graduate school at UMass, completed a master's degree in Latin Studies, and did some work toward a doctoral degree. Certified as a teacher, she took a job in the Holyoke public schools and, eventually, the Springfield schools. She taught second langue acquisition, basically teaching English to predominately Hispanic students.

Marjorie and her husband had a good marriage but after twenty-three years, their interests and needs had changed. When their boys were in their mid to late teens, they divorced. This was shortly before she and I met.

We began to date, fell in love, and moved in together in 1998. It has been a remarkable and joyful journey.

Marjorie is vivacious, warm, and almost overly sensitive to others. Her blond hair is graying, but she is in excellent health. Always a good athlete, she is slim and physically fit. Committed to social justice, Marjorie involves herself in protests and demonstrations. She also volunteers with Habitat for Humanity that recently included a return trip for her to Guatemala after forty years.

One of Marjorie's endearing qualities is her uncanny ability to meet and relate to others. While she enjoys her long-term relationships, and there are many, she quickly makes friends with strangers.

Once, we were in the hall of a hotel in which we were staying and ran into one of the housekeepers. Marjorie speaks fluent Spanish and began to talk to the woman who was from Guatemala. The woman talked of immigrating to this country, of having to leave her parents behind, and of the difficulties of her life here. After a long conversation, the two hugged having spent a precious moment of connection.

Marjorie and I enjoy the same things, especially our travels. We have been all over the world and particularly enjoy Southeast Asia. Once we trekked 180 miles in the independent Kingdom of Upper Mustang just below Lhasa, Tibet. There were no wheels, no running water, no electricity or any other amenities. We slept in tents and nine Sherpas helped us on the journey. We hiked through sunshine and snow. It was, by far, the best trip I have ever taken.

In the last few years, in addition to other destinations, we have been to Bhutan, Cambodia; the Caribbean; China; the Galápagos Islands; Nepal; Mexico; Morocco; Peru; Sicily; and Tibet. We were even stranded in Bali for three days when a volcano eruption interfered with air travel. For a while we owned a condominium in Snowmass, Colorado and often traveled there to ski.

We delight in socializing. While teahing, we especially liked to invite students to our home. One political science class came to watch a presidential debate between Hillary Clinton and Donald Trump.

Marjorie is the quintessential hostess. She is a gourmet cook and hardly a week goes by that we don't have friends visit for a meal. We are particularly popular in the summer when folks come to swim in the lake.

I love being with Marjorie. Sometimes I see her across a room and my heart tips. We share our thoughts and feelings. We seldom disagree and try to negotiate rather than argue. When we settle a difference through compromising, each of us believes we have received more from the other than we have given.

I feel safe and secure in the relationship knowing that neither of us will leave the other.

Marjorie continued to teach until her retirement in 2016, giving us more time to be with each other. Marjorie's sons are grown up and have turned into warm sensitive men. The oldest has two children – a girl, fifteen, and a boy, nine. They love coming to Nana's.

Chapter 32
Crossing Cultures

Now in my eighties, I realize with some surprise that I have lived more than half my life among the Yankees. How is the North so different from my sweet southern home, or is it? I have settled into a profession and a community. I have many friends, opportunities to travel, a wonderful relationship with my partner, and a nice home on a lake. Why would I ever miss the South?

Perhaps my memories are stirred by the great divisions in our country, such as those between conservatives and liberals, Blacks and whites, Northerners and Southerners. They have been particularly vivid for me in the controversies about flying the Confederate flag or removing statues of Confederate soldiers and in witnessing the impact of Black Lives Matter.

Growing up in Alabama and the panhandle of Florida, I cannot remember a time or place when the Confederate flag was not flying. Memory plays tricks in my mind. Was I really so proud of being a Southerner that the flag was always bright and unburnished? Could I truly have believed that the Civil War was about states right and not slavery? Did I really collect Confederate money and tearfully sing "Dixie?"

What is a poor southern kid to dream of if not the glory of the Old South and reclaiming a culture of honor?

I knew of the daring exploits of my Confederate soldier ancestors. How can I sustain this family history, especially after I have learned that the Confederate fighting was not a noble effort, but a desperate attempt to continue a way of life built on slavery?

I began to realize that states' rights were whatever you defined them to be and depended on where you lived. In Alabama, states' rights meant segregation and had nothing to do with civil rights.

So, what changed for me? How did I escape the worst of southern life? I do not know.

I do know, however, as I began to consider that I might be gay, that I was different, a secret that put me alongside the disadvantaged. Perhaps for that reason, I have always been drawn to the minority, those who do not fit into the overarching white, patriarchal majority.

I feel proud of having actively involved myself in all of the major social movements during my lifetime from civil rights through women's liberation, protests against the Vietnam War and the fight for LGBTQ rights. I still attend all of the local protests and occasionally march in national demonstrations. I like to think that my continued part in social action makes a difference.

I wonder how my life might have been different if I had remained in the South. I am sure I would have been active in the civil rights and women's movement, but opportunities for involvement in demonstrations and protests have been much more abundant in the Pioneer Valley.

I enjoy living in a liberal community among like-minded people. I love living in a semi-rural area beyond the urban realities of a large cities. The resources available to me through a great research university have enhanced my life in the academy.

If I had not moved, I doubt that I would be living in a lovely home on a lake. I would not have met my partner who nourishes and supports me, and is the love of my life.

Do I really cross cultures? Are Southerners and Northerners so different from each other?

I think so. Generally and politically, they seem miles apart in regard to embracing liberal versus conservative values.

Southerners seem more religious. I left the church in my middle teens. As a lesbian, I know I have been more accepted in the North. In the South, I would have lived in the closet for many more years. I have been able to live openly here in Massachusetts. Southerners seem to go about things more slowly than Northerners do. When asked a question, they will often answer with a long story. Everyone can notice the slow cadence of a southern accent. Southerners do appear to be friendlier than Northerners.

Just recently, I was talking to a Black staff woman in a hotel where I was staying in Birmingham. When we were finished chatting, she hugged me, something that would seldom happen where I live now.

Similarly, in Atlanta, when I moved into my home there I was immediately greeted by my neighbors. Here, after almost forty years of living in the same house, I still do not know my neighbors. But, perhaps I am just responding to New England "reserve."

I have many deep and abiding friendships here. Although I see prejudices against Blacks here in the North, Southerners overall may be more prejudiced toward people of color. Many are still fighting the Civil War under the guise of states' rights versus the federal government.

Finally, I now root for the Red Sox and the Patriots instead of the Braves and the Falcons. Perhaps for me the greatest change living in the North is that I no longer live under the shadow of the Civil War and I live openly as a lesbian.

As I have come to settle into life here, I feel I am finally able to relate to others without the prejudices toward Yankees that I once felt. I am often reminded of the South, especially in view of the racial divides in the country.

However, I am glad to be living quietly as a displaced Southerner who found a home in the North.

Chapter 33
Endings

Where have all the years gone? How many do I have left? Does anyone want to know the time of his or her death? Do I? I am not sure. Signs of mortality are all around me. As I age, now eighty-five, I am losing so many people.

My mentors are gone. My family is gone aside from my brother, Bud, his family, and a few cousins who are far away. Many of my best friends from college and early days have passed away. My senior tennis friends seem to be increasingly dying. Even some of my students have predeceased me. Several of my good friends have Alzheimer's. I miss a connection with folks who knew me well. Their passing continually reminds me of my own mortality.

Nevertheless, I do not want to dwell on past losses or failures or my obsessions and anticipatory anxieties about the future. Rather, I want to remember my life as one that is rich and rewarding.

I think of the mentors that changed my life – a neighbor that took me from the driveway of my home where I was hitting tennis balls against the wall to the County Club courts; the high school teacher who sent me to college; the psychology professor who helped me leave physical education to dwell in the world of ideas; my dissertation advisor who found me a job and the start of a professional career.

No doubt, growing up poor, a tomboy and eventually a lesbian were the major, if not the major impact in my life. From early on, I felt different from my friends. I could not name what was happening, but I maintained a staunch curiosity about my behavior and the behavior of others.

This curiosity remained with me all of my life and, perhaps, led me into psychology. I always wanted to know – and still do – how I fit in and how am I similar to and different from others? Especially, as I moved into adolescence, I knew that my attraction to other girls was different from that of my peers. Though I dated and tried to live a straight life, there was always a lurking understanding that something was not right.

I began to look around me to find whatever information I could about same-sex attraction. During those times, I quickly absorbed that being homosexual meant that one was a sexual pervert, a sinner and/or mentally ill. I suspected I was all three. It would be many years, almost half my life, before I could accept myself and eventually come to live authentically and openly as a lesbian.

What part did I play in my successes? I was bright and curious and somehow knew, even at an early age, that I especially enjoyed reading and writing. I loved books. They unfolded new worlds way beyond me and led me to dreams beyond my limited aspirations.

I loved school, a place where I was noticed and acknowledged. I delighted in good grades and impressing my teachers. I loved playing sports, all of them – softball, basketball, tennis, pick-up football and now pickleball. I entertained notions of becoming a tennis pro. I have had the good fortune of playing tennis throughout my life.

Probably to cover my insecurities, I presented a tough front. I tried to be independent and fearless. I never asked for help from anyone. I felt like I had to do everything for myself and never depend on others. This independence was probably helpful in some ways, but I know now how limiting it was. I did not know the comfort of being supported by others or the relief I could have found from letting others be helpful.

I was imbued with a work ethic from my early days. I was motivated and committed to my schoolwork. During graduate school days, I could have turned away from my new field of psychology about which I knew so little. However, my earlier schooling had shaped me, and I persevered. As always, I wanted to do well and impress my teachers.

In graduate school, I quickly involved myself into research and was among the first of my colleagues to present and publish my findings. As a university faculty member, I searched out research grants and, along with teaching, threw myself into research believing it to be the right thing to do.

I have always been a political junkie, a liberal, now a progressive Democrat. Addicted to the news, I was and still am alert to national and foreign affairs. I worry about our country. I wish there was more than I can do to change things for the better, especially for the disadvantaged and marginalized.

The students I have taught and continue to teach remain a great source of joy. I love to have them return to visit and I keep a special file of their thank you notes and letters. Some come back to my home to visit.

Just this last summer, I reconnected with an old student from Emory who came to visit after I had not seen her for fifty years. Recently, I had lunch with an old student who told me she had been in my class in 2006. After completing her Ph.D., she returned as a faculty member at UMass. My mechanic's wife, who runs their business, recognized me as an old faculty of hers when I first walked into her door. I also taught the nurse who is now my primary care provider. One of the students in my current class tells me I taught her father.

Further, I am deeply blessed with extraordinary friends. Our commitments to each other are deep and solid. They help me enjoy a myriad of pleasures ranging from a Saturday night movie to international travel.

My friends, straight and otherwise, are diverse but are probably overrepresented with professional women. I still feel like an imposter when I find myself at parties with authors and artists, doctors and deans, lawyers and judges. Within psychology, I feel even more out of place relating to famous scholars and distinguished researchers even as I know that students and younger colleagues are looking up to me.

My life feels balanced and seems simpler now. My classes are prepared so I can simply enjoy being with bright, energetic students when I teach.

When I sit in my living room and look around me, I am happy with the comfortable furniture, the paintings, and the collectibles I have garnered from around the world. I am content. I often sit on my deck looking out on the lake. Sometimes I read, sometime just sit silently. Mostly, I enjoy being with Marjorie.

The tattered Confederate flag still sits on my desk. I realize how confused and ambivalent I am about it.

It does remind me of my southern roots, but in the outside world, it is now a symbol of white supremacy and hate. Can I really bear the contradictions?

Perhaps it is time to fold it up and put it away.

Perhaps it is time for me to continue to reflect on its diverse meanings.

Perhaps, like my life, it is time to simply let it be.

MEMORIES

Top: Bonnie always enjoyed entertaining students at her home. Above: Taking a moment on her way to lobbying efforts in Washington, D.C . Left: Hiking in Colorado and feeling on top of the world.

THE GOOD LIFE

For nearly twenty-five years, Marjorie and Bonnie have been on a journey of love and joy. Their interests are many, including social justice activism. At right, Bonnie and Marjorie pose for a picture with the Capitol Building and its reflecting pool in the background following an LGBTQ march in Washington, D.C.

Acknowledgments

It takes a village to write a book. And, the inhabitants of my village were more than considerate and helpful. My thanks go to more of these people than I can express.

More than twenty years ago, Beverly Greene first encouraged me to write more autobiographical material. As editor of a book series, she published one of my first personal articles. I am grateful that she saw some substance in my writing and set me on the path to this book.

Across time, more friends and acquaintances than I can name read the manuscript and offered suggestions. Douglas Kimmel, Dusty Miller, Marilyn Patten, Norm Simonson, and the late Dennis Hinkle all wrote extensive comments on the book, which were extraordinarily helpful.

For about ten years, I attended a seminar called "Writing to Remember" sponsored by the Five College Learning in Retirement program. I am particularly grateful to the individuals in the group who listened carefully as members read their writings. They were always carefully critical and encouraging.

Having been raised calculating on stone tablets, I am computer phobic. Several extraordinary technical wizards helped with my every computer need – which was considerable. Chelsea Schurch introduced me to the advanced intricacies of the programs I was trying to run to complete the manuscript. She went well beyond my feeble attempts to use the computer. April Bellafiore and Sarah Winn were also valuable consultants in helping me through the computer maze. Cathy Jenson-Hole took over the sending of materials and photographs through cyberspace. Karin M. Camiholt spent too many Saturday mornings arranging and formatting the book.

I am grateful to Bridget Samburg, my careful editor. She made corrections to the manuscript and advised me on content. Some names were changed to protect privacy. I take responsibility for any mistakes.

When the manuscript was finished, I simply turned it over to Cindy Casey, publishing and literary consultant. Cindy is knowledgeable about all details of bringing a book to fruition. An ultimate professional, she took on more editing, formatting, designed a cover, sent out prepublications for review, and published the book. She was, and is, a steady source of advice and help. If you are holding the book in your hand or reading it electronically, it's because of Cindy.

And, I must acknowledge with affection and gratitude the continuing care and support I receive from my partner, Marjorie Nott. She encourages me in all of my undertakings and warms my heart.

Author's Note

As a psychologist and university professor, I have written, co-authored or co-edited more than a hundred book chapters, research articles, scholarly papers and a book in academic outlets. I was usually writing up research for journals that have instructions as to how to format the article. The composition of the article is primarily technical. It was only later in my professional career that I ventured into more autobiographical writing not expecting it to be published.

In the early 1990s, Beverly Green, a psychologist colleague from New York, was visiting me in Massachusetts and I shared some of my personal writing. As she returned home on the train, she read what I had written. On arriving home, she called and as editor of a book series, said she would like to publish what was to become the beginning of this book.

In 1997, Beverly published, *Leaving the Confederate Closet in Ethical and Cultural Issues Among Lesbians and Gay Men*. It was also reprinted (2001) in *Out in the South*, edited by C. Dewes and C. Law. Encouraged by this, I wrote several other personal pieces which were published – *A Faded Icon, A Butch among the Belles*, and *Beauty and the Butch*.

Across time, I continued to write this autobiographical book and in 2021 at age 85, I finished it. Many friends and acquaintances read the earlier drafts as did members of a seminar I took, "Writing to Remember," through our community Five College Learning in Retirement program. They encouraged me to publish the collective writings as a book.

This book, *Leaving the Confederate Closet: A Southern Les-*

bian's Journey, covers what I remember of my growing up days and my adulthood. I hope you enjoy it. If you want to comment on the book or just be in touch, you can find me on Facebook @BonnieStrickland, or you may contact me through email, bonnie@psych.umass.edu.